GEM TRAILS OF NEVADA

by
James R. Mitchell

Gem Guides Book Co.
315 Cloverleaf Dr., Suite F
Baldwin Park, CA 91706

Library of Congress Catalogue Number 91-077395
ISBN 0-935182-53-5

Cover Design: Bob Bates
Maps: Jean Hammond

INTRODUCTION

Nevada has long been known for its vast mineral deposits, and, in fact, the state's official nickname is "The Silver State." That mineral abundance, however, is not limited to commercial metals, but also to the plethora of other gemstones that can be gathered within its boundaries. If you choose to visit all of the sites discussed on the following pages, you will not only be able to gather an incredible variety of minerals and gems, but will also travel through landscapes with equally as much variety. You will collect among mighty pine trees on high mountain tops, desolate, parched deserts and virtually every type of terrain in between.

Detailed travel instructions are provided for each location, with an accompanying map and photo to assist with locating the sites. Mileages are as accurate as possible, but be advised that odometers on all vehicles vary and distances have been rounded to the nearest tenth of a mile.

It is important to note that the maps are intentionally NOT DRAWN TO SCALE. The purpose is to not only provide a general location setting, but to also better show travel detail near the site.

Some of the spots mentioned are situated on the dumps of old and abandoned mines. Do not, under any circumstances, enter the shafts and always be cautious when exploring surrounding regions. There are often hidden tunnels, rotten ground and pits, as well as rusty nails, broken glass and discarded chemicals, all of which create potential hazards.

A few places are on private property and access is not guaranteed or a fee may be charged to collect there. Fee information and land status is discussed as it was at the time of the author's most recent visit, shortly before publication, but DO NOT ASSUME THAT THIS GUIDE GIVES PERMISSION TO COLLECT! Land status changes frequently. If you have a suspicion that a particular site is no longer open, be sure to confirm that before entering. If nothing can be determined locally, land ownership information is usually available at the County Recorder's office.

The government regulates collecting petrified wood to no more than 25 pounds per day, plus one piece, and no more than 250 pounds per year. To obtain specimens weighing more than 250 pounds, a permit must be procured from the District Manager of the Bureau of Land Management. Groups cannot pool their allocations together to obtain pieces weighing more than 250 pounds and wood from public lands cannot be bartered or sold to commercial dealers and may only be gathered with hand tools.

Most of the areas discussed in the book are easy to get to, but road conditions do change. Severe weather can make good roads very rough and very rough roads totally impassable, even with four-wheel drive. You must decide for yourself on which of them your particular vehicle is capable of traveling.

Generally northern Nevada is wet and cold during the winter months, with the best collecting weather in the late spring, summer and early fall, even though it does get quite warm during the summer months. Southern

Nevada tends to be extremely hot during the summer, with the best collecting being in late fall, winter or early spring.

When venturing into some of the more remote areas, it is a good idea to take extra drinking water, foul weather clothing, a good map and even some food, just in case you get delayed or stuck. The Nevada Department of Transportation publishes an outstanding book, containing all 30', 15' and 7 1/2' planimetric maps in reduced size. The book is invaluable to anyone planning to spend a good amount of time exploring the backroads of Nevada, and is a handy companion to this book. The cost, at time of publication, is $12.00, which includes postage. For more information, write to the Nevada Department of Transportation, 1263 South Stewart Street, Room 206, Carson City, Nevada 89712, or call (702) 687-3451.

If you take the time to properly plan your trip and make sure your vehicle is in good working order, the gem fields listed on the following pages will provide you and your family with countless hours of pleasurable collecting, some outstanding mineral specimens, and many memorable experiences.

James R. Mitchell

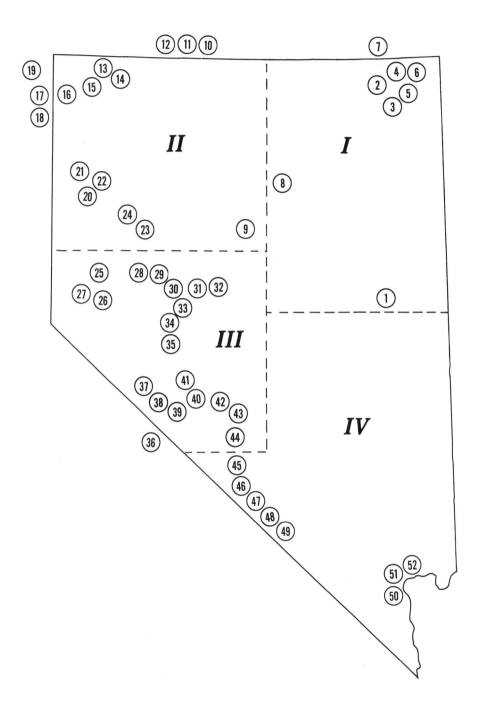

TABLE OF CONTENTS

SECTION I

SECTION II

SECTION III

SECTION IV

GARNET HILL

This location provides collectors an opportunity to gather dark red garnets. Many of the trapezohedral crystals are gem quality, but most are only specimen grade. Crystal size averages about 4mm across, although some have been found measuring as large as 15mm. Chunks of the host rhyolite containing a good number of well formed garnets, make great display pieces, especially if some of the garnets are large.

The garnets are best found in one of two ways. The most popular method is to break up the gray-pink rhyolite, which is scattered all over the hillside, in hopes of finding crystals in quartz-lined cavities. Secondly, however, many rockhounds have been very successful by screening or sifting through the light-colored soil, looking for specimens which have been weathered away from the host rock. The garnets of Garnet Hill are a deep red variety of almandine-spessartine, a manganese-aluminum variety of the gemstone.

To get to the base of the collecting area, follow instructions provided on the map. The turnoff from Highway 50 is well signed, and is situated just two-tenths of a mile west of where Highway 485 intersects. There are a few branching tracks along the way, but you should remain on the main road. One and six-tenths miles in from the pavement there is another sign indicating a right turn to the collecting site. From there, the road gets steep and narrow, making it inadvisable to take a motor home or trailer any further. Go another one and three-tenths miles to where there is a good place to pull off among the trees. The garnet-bearing rhyolite is just up the hill.

B.L. M. sign guiding the way to Garnet Hill

Garnet Hill

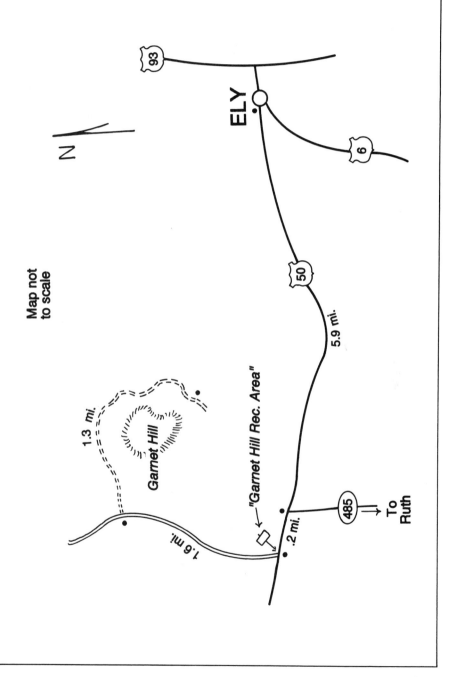

Map not to scale

93

ELY

6

50

5.9 mi.

1.3 mi.

Garnet Hill

"Garnet Hill Rec. Area"

1.6 mi.

.2 mi.

485

To Ruth

N

HUBBARD BASIN — WOOD

Some of the most colorful petrified wood to be found in the state of Nevada comes from Hubbard Basin. The colors, however, don't seem to be as vivid as those from Arizona's Petrified Forest, being in softer shades of blue, red, pink, yellow, purple, brown and white. Even though lots of collecting has been done here over the years, there is still some material left. However, it is much tougher to find, especially in larger sizes. A few years ago, the B.L.M. allowed commercial collectors to bulldoze the area, and that significantly depleted the supply.

There is still some wood available for those willing to do hard digging, and it could be well worth your time and effort, if already in the area, to try your luck. In addition to the pleasing colors, many pieces have retained their original wood structure, including knots and worm holes. Occasionally a lucky rockhound will unearth spectacular logs or branches with crystal lined interiors. Those are the most ardently sought specimens from this locality.

There are lots of small chips of colorful wood scattered about on the surface throughout the region, but the best digging tends to be restricted to the hillsides. Look for pits left by previous rockhounds for indications as to where to start your excavation.

To get to Hubbard Basin, take Highway 93 about 30 miles south from Jackpot to O'Neil Road, where you should turn west and proceed three and nine-tenths miles. At that point, leave the main road, going right onto the much rougher ruts. Follow those ruts seven and one-half miles to the collecting area, which is easy to spot, by the diggings on the hill and the bulldozed regions left by the commercial collectors. Do not travel to Hubbard Basin if the roads are wet, since the roadbed is composed of clay that becomes very slick and sticky. Even four-wheel drive units have been known to get severely stuck. In addition, due to deep rutting, a high clearance vehicle is mandatory. Be sure to read about B.L.M. restrictions governing collecting petrified wood in the introduction to this book.

Sign at the turnoff from Highway 93

Hubbard Basin

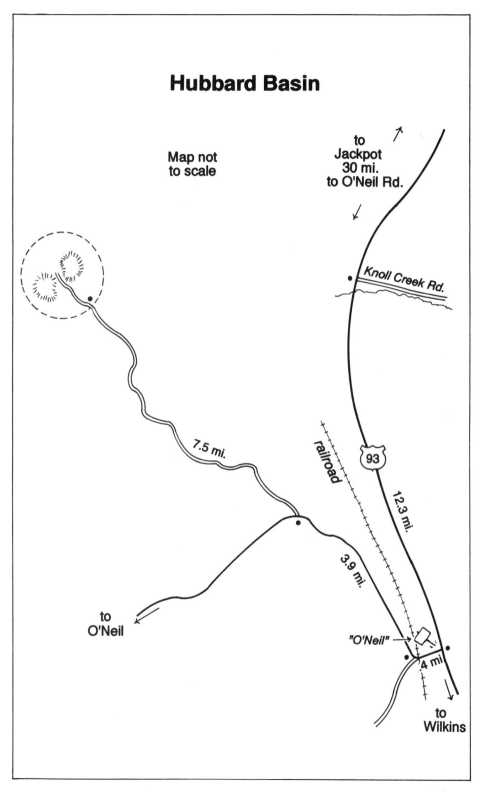

Map not
to scale

to
Jackpot
30 mi.
to O'Neil Rd.

Knoll Creek Rd.

railroad

93

7.5 mi.

12.3 mi.

3.9 mi.

to
O'Neil

"O'Neil"

.4 mi

to
Wilkins

CONTACT — MINERALS

This site offers the collector specimen grade chrysocolla and malachite, and the possibility of finding an occasional crystal-filled geode. To get there, take Highway 93 sixteen miles south from Jackpot to the small town of Contact. From there, continue one and four-tenths miles to a dirt road that can be seen heading off to the east. Follow that road two-tenths of a mile, bear left at the fork and follow the tracks paralleling the Little Salmon River. Continue one and five-tenths miles to the gray dirt mounds. It is in this area that geodes are reported to have been found. However, the author has not been successful in locating any. Search the mound area and do some digging, maybe you will have better luck.

Continue along the road to the mine, which can easily be seen from the mounds. The old workings and cabin afford a picturesque setting within which rockhounds can gather specimens of vivid green and blue malachite and chrysocolla. Most is not thick enough to polish, and is only suitable for display in mineral collections. However, the color tends to be good. Be sure to stay out of the mine shaft, since there are a number of vertical drops which could be very dangerous if inadvertently stepped into. Some showy crystal cavities have been found in and around the mine dumps and it might be worth your time to do a little rock splitting, in hopes of exposing such prizes. If it appears the mine is no longer abandoned when you visit, do not collect there.

Cabin and mineshaft near collecting site

Contact Minerals

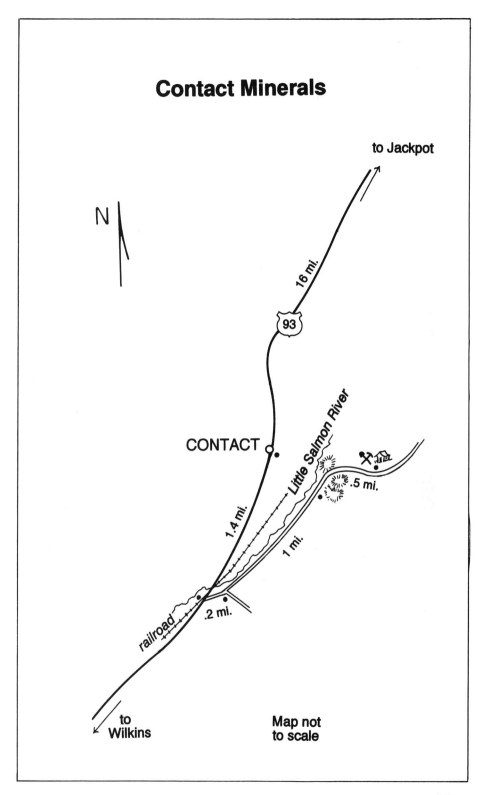

to Jackpot

N

16 mi.

93

CONTACT

Little Salmon River

.5 mi.

1.4 mi.

1 mi.

railroad

.2 mi.

to
Wilkins

Map not
to scale

TEXAS SPRING — LIMB CASTS

Texas Spring limb casts are prized by collectors from all over the country. The beautiful pink agate inherent to those casts can be used to produce fantastic cabochons and other polished pieces.

This location has been known among rockhounds for years. The supply has been somewhat depleted, but the site still rewards diligent collectors willing to dig and spend some time. Lots of agate chips can be found scattered on the surface, but prize pieces displaying the original structure of contorted and twisted roots or limbs cast in pink and red agate, are obtained only by digging.

It is generally necessary to get about 18 inches below the surface with pick and shovel before starting to encounter anything worthwhile, but the soil isn't too tough to excavate and the casts are somewhat plentiful. Luck plays a most important part in your success. The casts tend to be only about four to six inches long and no more than two inches across.

In addition, delicate and beautiful tiny pink agate twigs can be collected on the surface, mainly alongside the road. Most have a thin white coating or a "snake skin" crackled white exterior, both of which can usually be removed by light tumbling.

This is a remote spot, so be certain your vehicle is in good working order and you have plenty of supplies in the event you are delayed. Be also advised that there are many intersecting roads along the way. Stay on the main thoroughfare, as shown on the map, and you should have no problems. If things don't seem to be happening according to the map, it might be necessary to double back a short distance and try again.

Sign along Highway 93 designating the turnoff

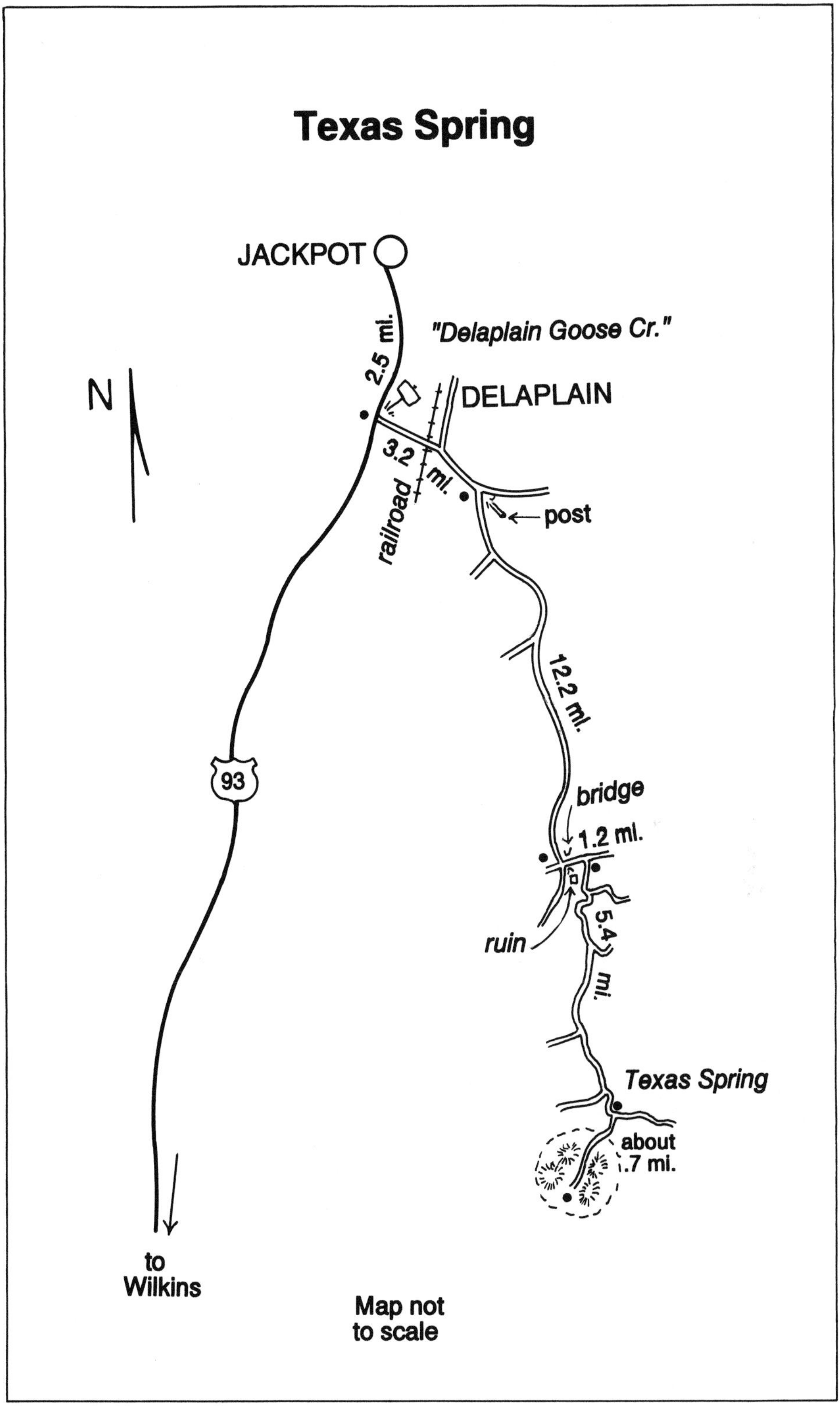

Texas Spring

JACKPOT ○

2.5 ml.

"Delaplain Goose Cr."

DELAPLAIN

N

railroad

3.2 ml.

post

12.2 ml.

93

bridge

1.2 ml.

ruin

5.4 ml.

Texas Spring

about
.7 mi.

to
Wilkins

Map not
to scale

BOGWOOD DIGGINGS — PETRIFIED WOOD

The two sites described here are both reached by heading south on Highway 93 from Jackpot to the Delaplain turnoff, about two and one-half miles from town. Go east three and two-tenths miles and bear right at the fork twelve and two-tenths miles, being certain to remain on the main road. At the given mileage, turn left, cross a wooden bridge, and proceed one and two-tenths miles, then go right another two and eight-tenths miles. At that point, there will be a road leading right. Drive onto that road a short distance to where diggings can be seen throughout the brush and juniper covered hills. That is Site "A".

It is there that you can obtain nice bogwood, petrified wood and an occasional limb cast. Colors include white, pink and brown, usually mixed together to produce very desirable patterns and contrasts. The most sizeable material is found by digging a foot or more in the whitish bentonite ash, even though smaller chunks are scattered about the surface throughout the area.

Snakeskin agate can be acquired at Site "B", which is reached by returning to the main road and going south another nine and one-tenth miles to the intersection with Rock Springs Road. This unusual cutting material can be found for quite a distance through the hills to the northeast of the intersection. The agate isn't too tough to spot, having a distinctive tubular shape, with a generally whitish, crackled exterior. Don't let this nondescript surface fool you. Some of the interiors are very nice, frequently being filled with unusual inclusions. Be careful to select only the best offered here, since some is very porous and unable to take a high polish. Don't hesitate to do some walking among the brush, and it may also be productive to do a little digging in suspect areas.

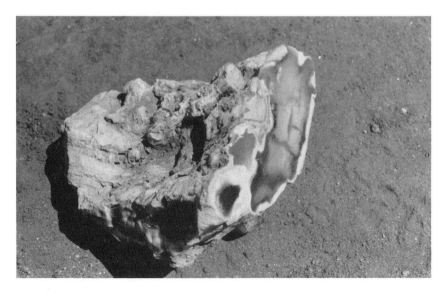

Specimen found at Bogwood Diggings

Bogwood

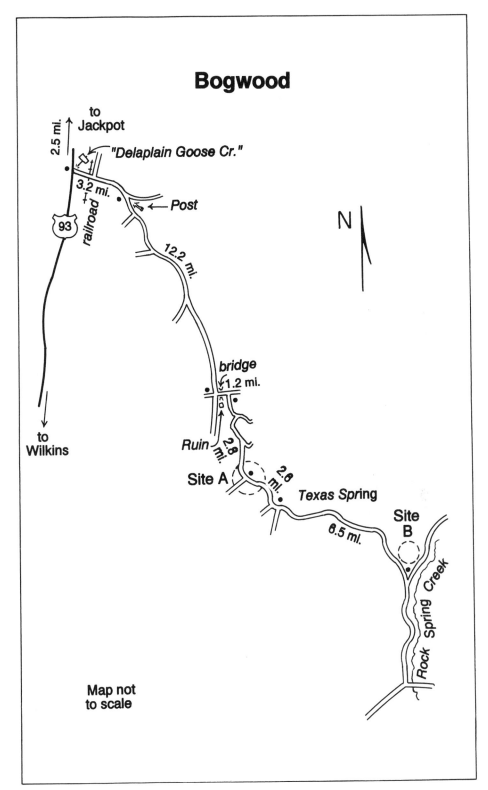

to
Jackpot

2.5 mi.

"Delaplain Goose Cr."

3.2 mi.

railroad

93

Post

12.2 mi.

to
Wilkins

N

bridge

1.2 mi.

Ruin

2.8 mi.

Site A

2.6 mi.

Texas Spring

Site
B

6.5 mi.

Rock Spring Creek

Map not
to scale

JACKPOT — ONYX

This location offers rockhounds lots of good quality banded onyx, as well as a scenic drive through the back country of northeastern Nevada. To get there from Jackpot, go south from town on Highway 93 about two and one-half miles to the Delaplain and Goose Creek turnoff. Follow that road east three and two-tenths miles and then bear right at the fork, continuing another nine and four-tenths miles. As you approach the proper mileage, the mine can be seen on the mountainside. Turn left, cross the little creek, and go around the ruins of the old onyx shop, as shown on the map. Proceed along the often steep and rutted road, as it winds its way to the dumps. If the road is wet do not attempt this drive, even with four-wheel drive since it traverses many stretches of clay and gumbo that can be very treacherous.

If you are not sure whether your vehicle can climb the hill, it is advisable to hike rather than drive. There aren't many good places to turn around once starting up, so don't attempt anything you may regret. Most trucks and rugged vehicles should have no problems if driven carefully and the road is dry.

The onyx can be found on the hillsides below the mine, on the dumps and along the road as you approach. The quality varies greatly, but tends to be good. It doesn't take long to find some fine specimens. Since the material is so desirable, the mine has been reactivated from time to time over the years. For that reason, be certain that the workings are still abandoned at the time you visit. If you have any questions as to whether collecting is allowed, be satisfied with what can be found in the lower areas.

Jackpot Onyx

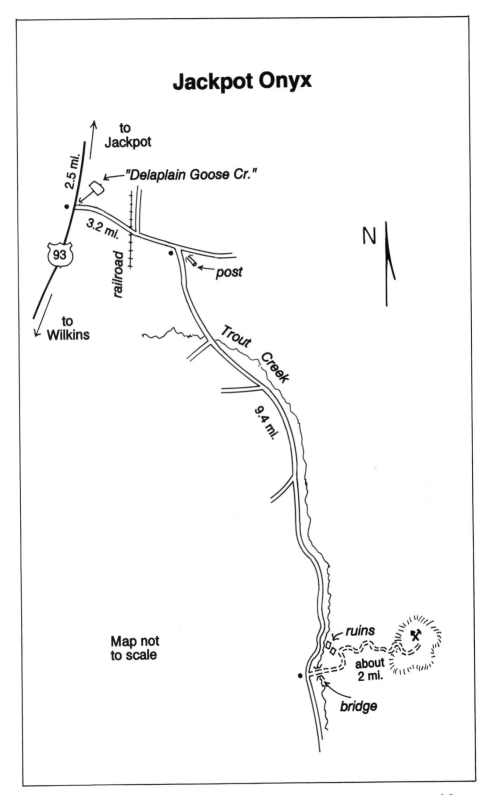

RABBIT SPRINGS — NODULES

Small geodes and nodules can be found a short distance north of Jackpot, in the hills east of the highway. To get there, take Highway 93 north from town five and one-tenth miles to the Rabbit Springs Recreation Area turnoff. To help spot the turn, look for the Bureau of Land Management sign just off the pavement on the right. Follow the road through the rest area to the base of the hills, about two-tenths of a mile. The geodes and nodules can be found throughout the basalt ridges and in the lowlands below.

This site has been known for years, and due to its close proximity to the major highway, the easily accessible regions have been virtually picked clean. It is now necessary to walk a distance to find any worthwhile quantities of the geological oddities. They occur as part of the basalt, in the form of crusted bubbles clinging to areas of decomposition, or loose in the soil throughout the lowlands, having been weathered from where they were formed in the upper ridges.

Walk through areas of erosion and you should be able to spot lots of chips and pieces, as well as some complete spherical specimens, most of which are no more than two or three inches in diameter. It shouldn't take much time to gather quite a few of the little orbs if you are willing to patiently trek some distance from the highway. Be advised that a large percentage of the nodules are duds filled with nothing more than porous rhyolite. The prizes, however, have beautiful agate centers, some with glistening crystal filled cavities.

View of the collecting site facing east

Rabbit Springs

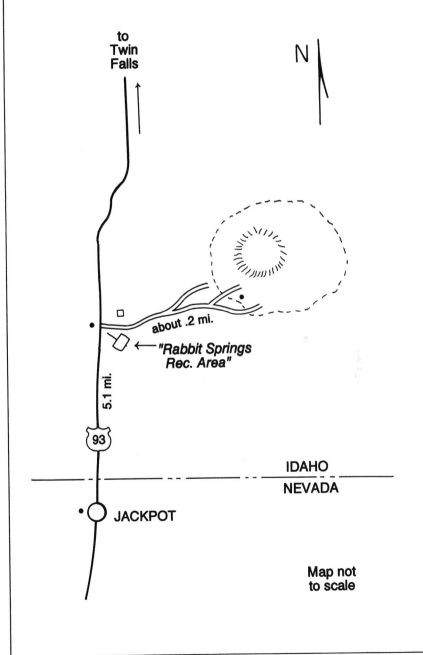

to
Twin
Falls

N

about .2 mi.

← "Rabbit Springs
Rec. Area"

5.1 mi.

93

IDAHO
NEVADA

JACKPOT

Map not
to scale

PALISADE — AGATE

This is the site of an abandoned mine dump. As is the case at all mines, there is always the possibility that the mine could become active again. Be certain that the mine is still abandoned when you visit. If there is any indication that collecting is not allowed, avoid doing so. In addition, always be careful in regard to stepping on nails or glass, and do not ever enter a shaft no matter how stable it may appear.

To get to this interesting collecting location, take Highway 278 south from Carlin eight and seven-tenths miles to the Palisade turnoff. There is a difficult-to-spot sign alongside the pavement, so be on the lookout as you approach. Proceed west one-half mile and then bear right across the railroad tracks one-tenth of a mile. From there, follow the tracks another two and three-tenths miles to the dumps, which will be seen as you approach.

These dumps offer the collector lots of jasper and jasp-agate in a variety of colors and patterns. Scattered about is bright green, yellow and gold material, some with showy black stringers and other inclusions. The jasp-agate is especially interesting but not very abundant.

Be advised that much of what can be found here is porous, making it mandatory to allow sufficient time for finding quality material. Carefully examine chunks with the brightest and most saturated color, since those generally tend to be the most solid and offer a much greater potential for taking a good polish.

Ruins at the mine site

Palisade

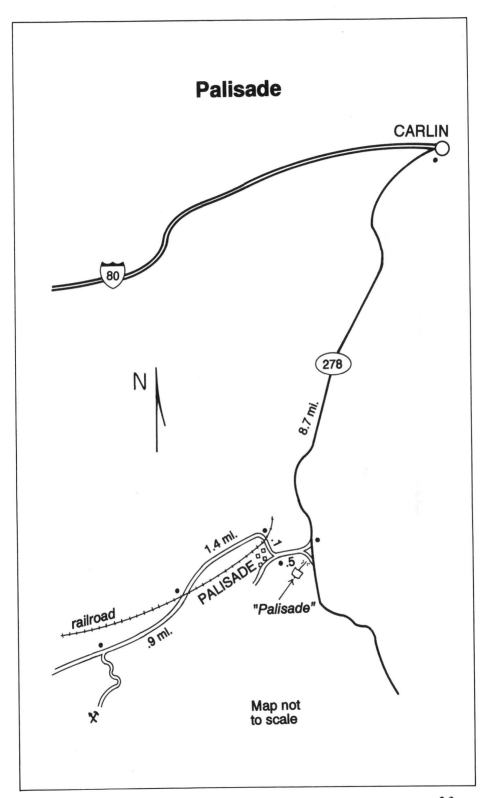

CARLIN

80

278

8.7 mi.

N

1.4 mi.

.1

PALISADE

.5

"Palisade"

railroad

.9 mi.

X

Map not
to scale

DAISY CREEK — WOOD

This site is frequently called Dacie Creek, but official topographic maps refer to it as Daisy Creek. The location has been known by Nevada rockhounds for many years. Due to the large amount of collecting that has taken place, diligent digging and a little luck are now required in order to find sizeable specimens of the colorful petrified wood that has given the place such distinction.

To get to this somewhat remote spot, proceed ten miles south from Battle Mountain on Highway 305 and then bear right where there is a sign alongside the pavement designating the turn toward the town of Galena. The Galena road turns to gravel after about two miles, but it is fairly well graded most of the way to the site. Go 22 miles from the highway and then turn left toward Daisy Creek Ranch. Continue about six more miles and then start looking for indications, on either side of the road that previous collectors have been digging. This is a somewhat extensive site, and excavations will be seen for quite a distance.

Chips and small specimens can be found in the existing mounds and tailings, and these regions serve as good indicators as to where you should consider working if you decide to dig. Look for spots with a good concentration of chips to help guide you to the most potentially prolific terrain. Since this is ranch land, holes should be refilled before leaving to prevent injury to cattle and other wildlife.

Daisy Creek

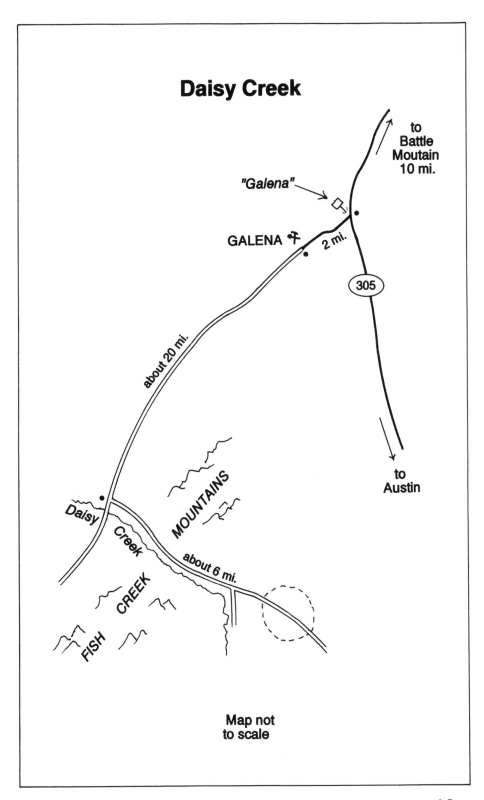

to
Battle
Moutain
10 mi.

"Galena"

GALENA ✝

2 mi.

305

about 20 mi.

to
Austin

Daisy

Creek

MOUNTAINS

about 6 mi.

FISH CREEK

Map not
to scale

MCDERMITT — WONDERSTONE

Intricately patterned and banded rhyolite, often referred to as wonderstone, can be found in the hills northwest of McDermitt. To get to the primary collecting site from town, go west four and three-tenths miles to a sign indicating the road to Disaster Peak. At that point, turn north, travel about one-tenth of a mile around the gravel pit, and then proceed left fourteen miles as the road winds its way westward.

As you approach the given mileage, lots of pits and associated rubble will be seen, primarily on the left. This marks the center of the wonderstone deposit. Look through the various excavations to ascertain exactly what can be found and either gather wonderstone from the tailings or do some digging directly into the hard rock, extracting material from regions which appear to offer the most potential.

Procuring the tough rhyolite from its place in the ground involves hard work, but the rewards can be well worth the effort. Some of this fascinating stone displays nice scenic "pictures", while other samples are simply filled with bands and swirls. The finest exhibit very high contrast and will take a dull polish.

Be advised that much of what can be found here is very grainy, so it takes a concerted effort to find pieces that will have good lapidary applications. Some of the more porous material, though is so unusual that it still might be usable for producing larger items such as bookends and clock faces where a quality polish isn't mandatory.

There are a number of mining claims in the general area, so be sure to restrict your collecting to regions outside these claims!

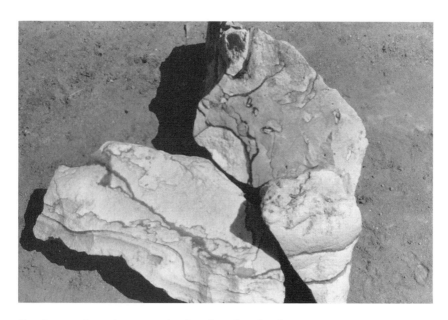

Specimens of wonderstone (rhyolite) found at the site

McDermitt Wonderstone

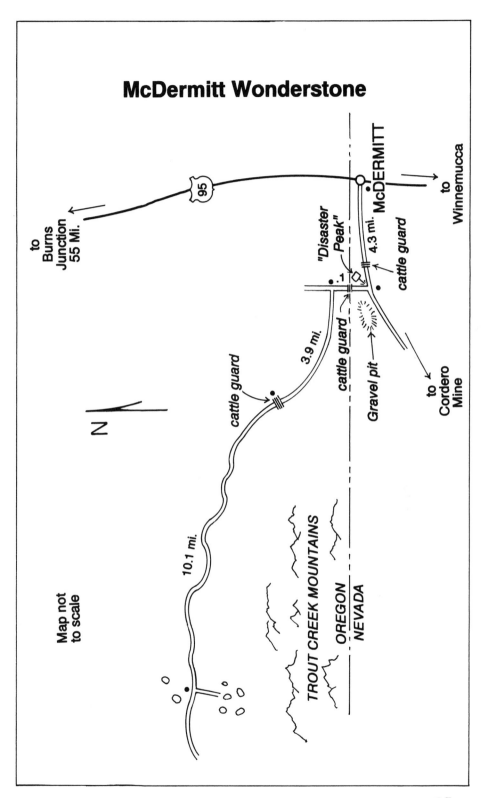

MCDERMITT MINERALS

The three sites illustrated on the map offer rockhounds petrified wood, chert, agate, wonderstone and jasper. To get to the first site, Site "A", go four and three-tenths miles west of town to the Disaster Peak turnoff. Proceed right one-tenth of a mile and then left seven and three-tenths miles to a road leading off to the right. Follow that road about seven-tenths of a mile to the center of a collecting area where you can pick up generally small, but frequently well formed chunks of petrified wood. In addition, Site "A" offers rockhounds brilliant white chert, agate and colorful jasper. Pay particularly close attention to areas of erosion, looking for specimens that have been partially uncovered. To find the largest material, you will probably have to do some random digging. If you choose to do so, be sure to refill your holes to prevent injury to cattle and other wildlife.

To get to the next sites, return to the main road and continue west another six and four-tenths miles. Turn right and go through the gate, being sure to close it after passing through. Drive one-tenth of a mile further, and then follow the ruts up the side of the hill to the easily seen diggings that mark the center of Site "B". Within the region surrounding the quarry one can find lots of swirled rhyolite, often referred to as wonderstone, and opalite, some of which is mixed into the interesting host rock. Good specimens can be extracted from the place in the cliff or from the rubble below. It appears that this quarry has long been abandoned, but if there is any indication otherwise, restrict your search to areas below.

Follow the road, as shown on the map, another one and one-half miles to Site "C". Numerous pits will be seen on both sides of the road, and it is in and around those pits that collectors can gather colorful jasper, petrified wood and banded rhyolite. The wood tends to be gray and tan, but often displays its ancient structure exquisitely. The jasper occurs in a variety of colors, most predominantly orange and red.

The quarry at Site "B"

McDermitt Minerals

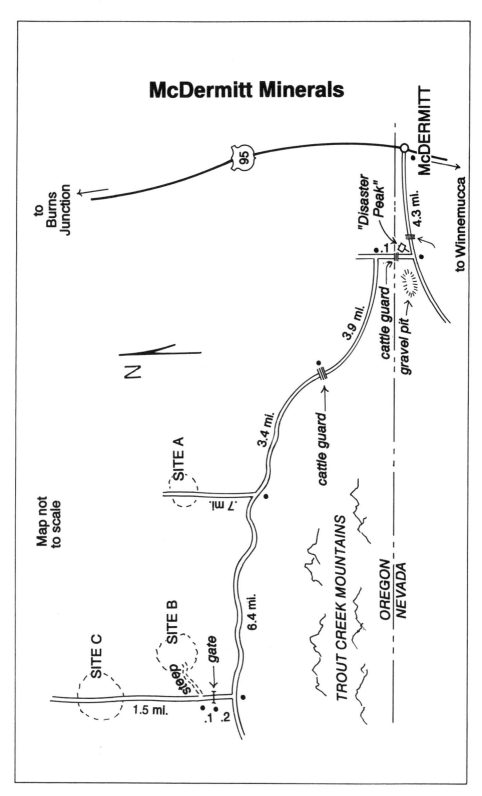

MCDERMITT — PETRIFIED WOOD

Even though this location is actually in Oregon, the only access is through Nevada, and it offers collectors fine specimens of petrified wood, some of which can be very sizeable. The dirt road leading to the site is well graded and should present no difficulty to most vehicles. In fact, passenger cars should be able to make the trip if driven carefully.

The wood location is extensive and lots of surface material can be found within the region shown on the map, especially at the now abandoned mine. It is necessary to dig for the largest and best-preserved specimens. However, hard work is usually rewarded with some fine petrified wood. Chunks of limbs and even complete tree trunks have been found here, most of which faithfully replicates the wood's original structure in incredible detail.

If you decide to do some digging, be sure to have a pick, shovel, gloves and plenty of energy. The entire area is filled with pits where previous rockhounds have worked, and it is suggested that you use those excavations as a guide in determining where to start.

This is a prolific location, and it takes little effort to gather a good quantity of nice petrified wood. Some colorful chunks of agate and jasper can also be picked up, so be on the lookout for those highly desirable collectibles. It is so easy to become overwhelmed by the quality of wood, that rockhounds often overlook the beautiful supplementary minerals.

Don't forget that the government restricts collectors to gathering no more than 25 pounds of wood per day, with a maximum of 250 pounds in any year. If you unearth a piece weighing more that 250 pounds and would like to see it displayed in a museum or similar institution, a permit for its removal can be requested through the Bureau of Land Management.

Specimens of petrified wood found at the site

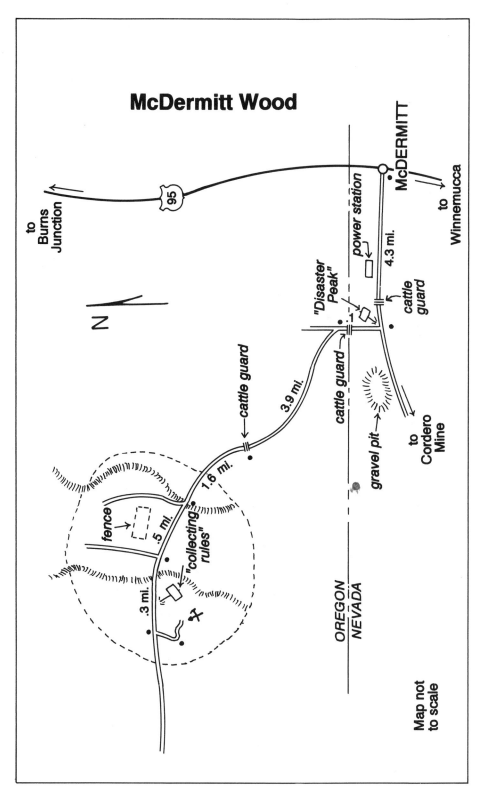

McDermitt Wood

to Burns Junction

95

N

to Winnemucca

McDERMITT

"Disaster Peak"

power station

cattle guard

4.3 mi.

.1

cattle guard

3.9 mi.

cattle guard

gravel pit

to Cordero Mine

1.6 mi.

fence

.5 mi.

"collecting rules"

.3 mi.

OREGON
NEVADA

Map not to scale

31

DENIO — MINERALS

This site features lots of small Apache tears, yellow and gold jasper, and some beautiful orange opalite as well as occasional pieces of carnelian.

Denio Junction, on the Nevada-Oregon border, can be reached via U.S. Highway 91 and State Highway 140. To get to the collecting site from Denio Junction, simply head west on Highway 140 approximately 25 miles to the turnoff to Virgin Valley. There is a Bureau of Land Management sign just off the pavement that you should concentrate on locating as you approach since the road is windy. If you miss it, turning around on this stretch of highway is not only hazardous but, also, difficult.

Proceed south toward Virgin Valley, but park just after leaving the pavement on any of the flat terrain beside the gravel road. Search in any direction on either side of the highway, as far as you like. Specimens tend to be small and they are scattered for quite a distance, with an especially good concentration being near the hills north of the highway.

The orange opalite stands out vividly against the light colored soil, as do the countless Apache tears. The jasper and carnelian are a little more scarce and difficult to locate, but with patience you should be able to gather a worthwhile quantity in a short amount of time.

As you drive to either of the two precious opal mines discussed on the following pages, be sure to stop at some of the numerous, colorful, badlands-like dirt mound areas encountered along the way. Most cream-colored opal from this region fluoresces a brilliant green under short wave ultraviolet lamps. When exploring these sites, however, be sure you don't trespass on any valid claims.

Collecting north of the highway near the hills

Denio Minerals

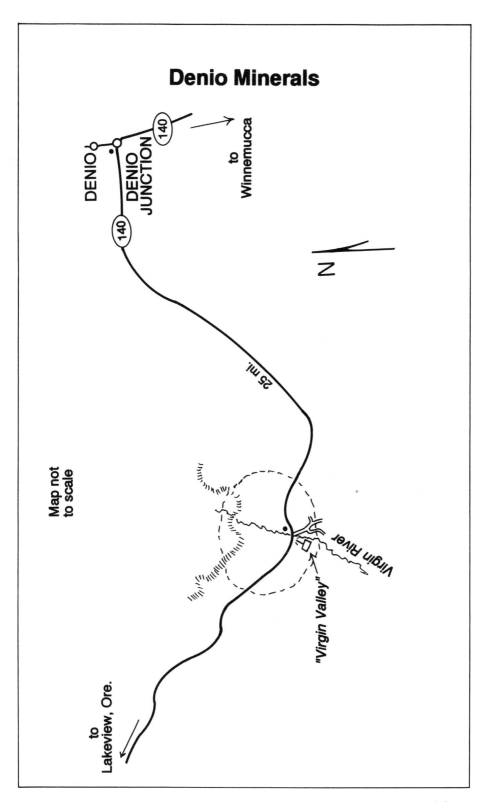

RAINBOW RIDGE PRECIOUS OPAL

The Rainbow Ridge Precious Opal Mine is one of only two prospects in renowned Virgin Valley open to amateur collectors. To get there, go 25 miles west from Denio Junction on Highway 140 to where a Bureau of Land Management sign designates the turnoff. Proceed south two and one-half miles to the CCC campground and then follow the signs to Rainbow Ridge.

At time of publication the mine was open annually from Memorial Day until the first of October, and collectors are charged a per person, per day fee to explore the tailings in hopes of unearthing some of the most spectacular precious opal to be found anywhere in the world. Collectors at Rainbow Ridge do not dig directly into the opal bearing strata, because of its inaccessability. Instead, the owner strips away the approximate thirty feet of overburden with a D-8 cat and then pushes the opal bearing clay onto the dumps. This is a most efficient method of bypassing the time consuming job of breaking down the host soil, and the results have proven to be very good.

Collectors are advised to bring their own tools, including a small garden rake, shovel or trowel, spray bottle for water, gloves, hat and sunscreen.

There is a small rockshop on the premises, and opal is for sale there. It is advisable, whether you plan to purchase anything or not, to drop by the shop and examine specimens of what can be found at the mine. Knowing what you are looking for greatly enhances your chances for success.

The mine is open five days a week, being closed on Tuesdays and Thursdays so the management can replenish the tailings with fresh material. Hours of operation are from 8 A.M. until 4 P.M. For more information, contact the Rainbow Ridge Mine before April 24th at Hodson's of Scottsdale, Inc., 7116 First Avenue, Scottsdale, AZ 85251, (602) 945-2262; and between May 26th and October 1st at Box 97, Denio, Nevada 89404, (702) 941-0270.

A view of the hills near the Rainbow Ridge Mine

Rainbow Ridge Opal Mine

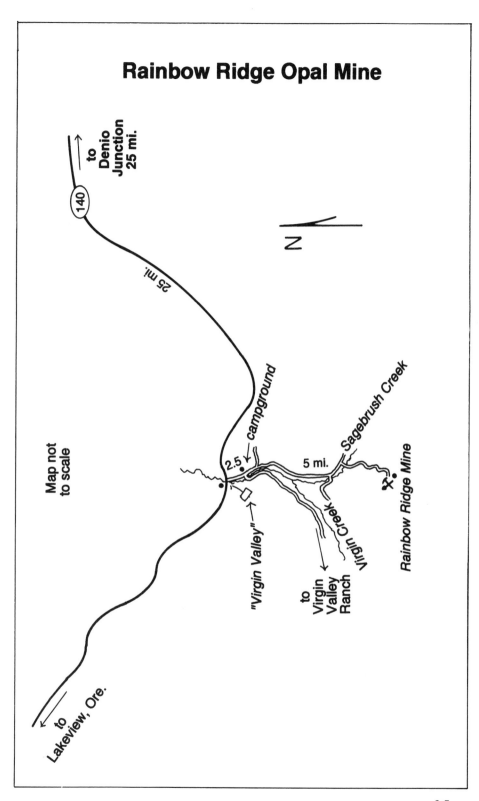

to Denio Junction 25 mi.

140

25 mi.

Map not to scale

N

campground

2.5

5 mi.

Sagebrush Creek

Rainbow Ridge Mine

Virgin Creek

"Virgin Valley"

to Virgin Valley Ranch

to Lakeview, Ore.

ROYAL PEACOCK PRECIOUS OPAL

Of the more than 150 mining claims staked in the world-famous Virgin Valley, this is one of the two which are open to amateur collectors. The valley boasts some of the finest precious opal to be found anywhere, including Australia, and having the opportunity to find specimens of that incredibly colorful gemstone is a dream come true for many mineral collectors. To get to the mine, follow Highway 140 west from Denio Junction about 25 miles to the Bureau of Land Management sign designating the turnoff. Go south two and one-half miles to the CCC campground, and then right, toward the Virgin Valley Ranch, another seven miles. At that point, there is a sign designating the turnoff to the Royal Peacock Mine, and from there, the office is one mile further. It is essential that you stop at the office before going to the mine itself, in order to pay the fee and get last minute instructions.

Rockhounds should have a minimum of the following: shovel, rake, small trowel, rock pick, spray bottle with water, hat, sunscreen, first aid supplies and gloves.

At time of publication, the mine is open from the middle of May through September, from 8 A.M. until 4 P.M., seven days a week. You can search through the tailings for a reduced fee or attack the opal bearing clay itself, for a slightly higher price. The latter is tough and time consuming work, but the rewards can be incredible.

The Royal Peacock offers full R.V. hookups and there are also two furnished trailers on the site. If you would like to reserve a space or rent one of the trailers, it is suggested you communicate with the mangement well ahead of time. For further information, contact the Royal Peacock Opal Mine, Inc., at P.O. Box 55, Denio, Nevada 89404, or call (702) 941-0374.

Collecting at the Royal Peacock Mine

Royal Peacock Opal Mines

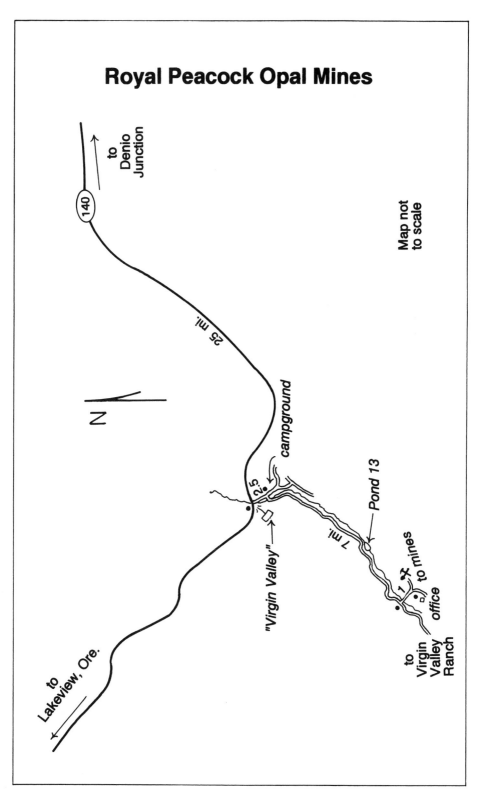

to Denio Junction

140

25 mi.

Map not to scale

N

campground

2.5

"Virgin Valley"

Pond 13

7 mi.

to mines

office

1

to Virgin Valley Ranch

to Lakeview, Ore.

BIG SPRINGS OBSIDIAN

The region between Highway 140 and Cedarville is covered with top quality gem obsidian and Apache tears. In fact, along some stretches of the gravel road shown on the map, the soil is black due to the heavy obsidian concentration. Four specific sites are discussed here, but actually anywhere along this road affords good collecting possibilities.

Site "A" boasts a concentration of obsidian and Apache tears. The field starts about three miles from where A-34 intersects Highway 140 and it encompasses at least two more miles. Simply stop anywhere within the given mileage to gather as much as you desire. Some is more transparent than others, so take time to find the best. If you chose to split any specimens, in order to ascertain quality and transparency, be sure to wear protective goggles and gloves. When struck with a hammer, the volcanic glass sends needle-like splinters flying through the air.

Another Apache tear and obsidian field is located about two miles beyond the fork, as shown on the map. This is Site "B", also quite extensive. Site "C" is somewhat unusual, featuring a light-weight, porous, ash rock which may be a type of perlite, containing tiny Apache tears. A hillside of this unique, grayish material will be seen on the left side of the road at the given mileage. Pieces filled with Apache tears partially embedded are very nice for display in a mineral collection. Moonstone is also reported to have been found here, so be on the lookout.

To get to Site "D", bear right at the fork just past Site "C", and go about eight more miles. This will place you in the center of yet another obsidian and Apache tear field which extends at least four more miles. Additional obsidian will be encountered all the way to Cedarville.

Parked at Site "A"

Big Springs Obsidian

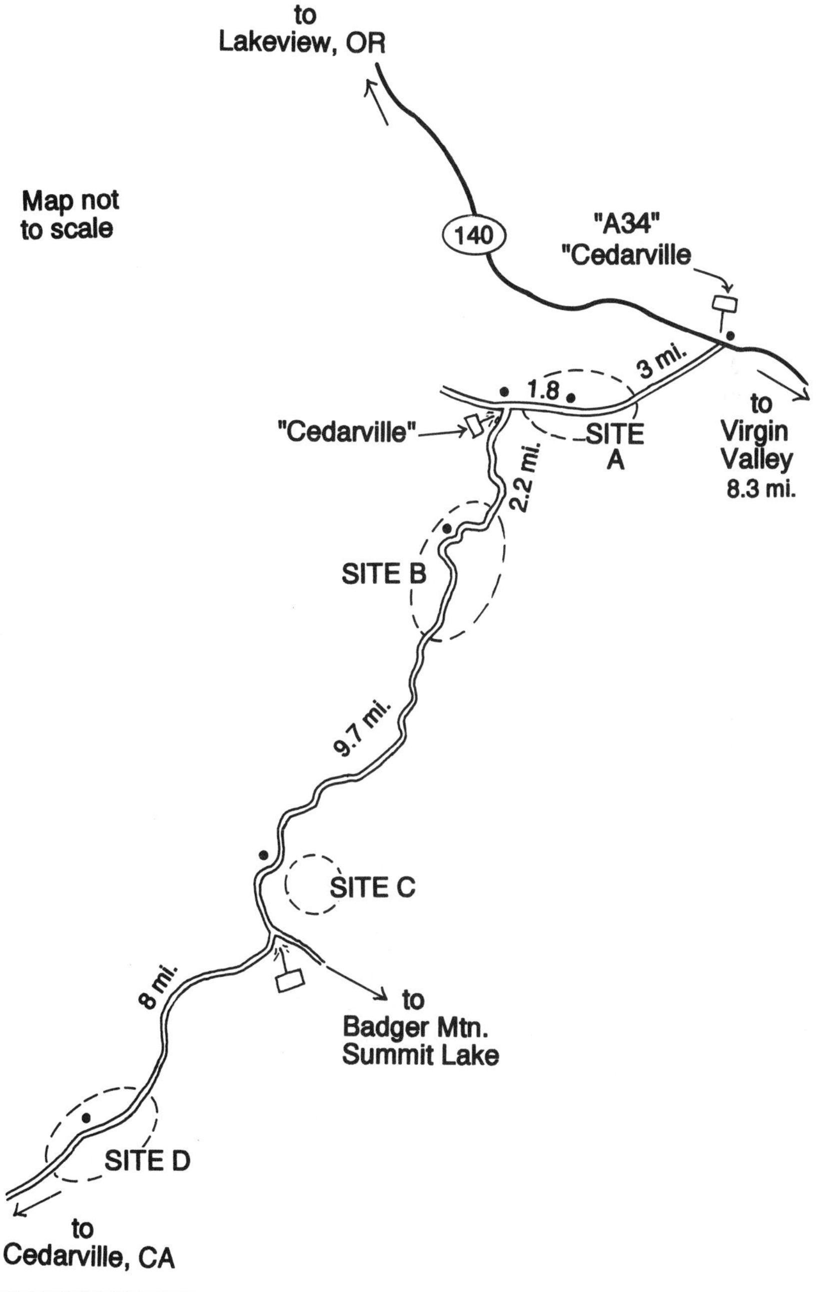

to
Lakeview, OR

Map not
to scale

140

"A34"
"Cedarville

"Cedarville"→

1.8

3 mi.

SITE
A

to
Virgin
Valley
8.3 mi.

2.2 mi.

SITE B

9.7 mi.

SITE C

to
Badger Mtn.
Summit Lake

8 mi.

SITE D

to
Cedarville, CA

CEDARVILLE SOUTH

Lots of petrified wood can be found south of Cedarville, California, only a short distance west of the Nevada border. To get to Site "A", go south from town about four miles to Granger Creek Road, turn right and proceed another four miles. The wood is scattered throughout the hills to the north about one city block from where you park. Simply roam the lowlands looking for the wood, either partially buried or as surface chips. Pay particularly close attention to regions of erosion, in hopes of discovering more sizeable pieces. Most of what is found here and at the other two sites, are specimen quality only, and rarely colorful and/or solid enough for polishing. Much, however, is ideal for display in a mineral collection.

To get to Site "B", return to Highway 34 and continue south another four and two-tenths miles to where you will see a gravel pit on the east side of the road. Just a short distance further the road dips and crosses a large wash. That is the collecting area. Hike through the wash in either direction to gather additional petrified wood and even some nice bloodstone. The best time to collect here is after a good rainstorm, since that tends to clean the rocks, making stones of interest easier to spot.

Site"C" is reached by traveling an additonal four miles south on Highway 34 to another wash. Fine specimen quality petrified wood can be found there, but it is necessary to hike a distance to the west from the highway in order to find the best the location has to offer.

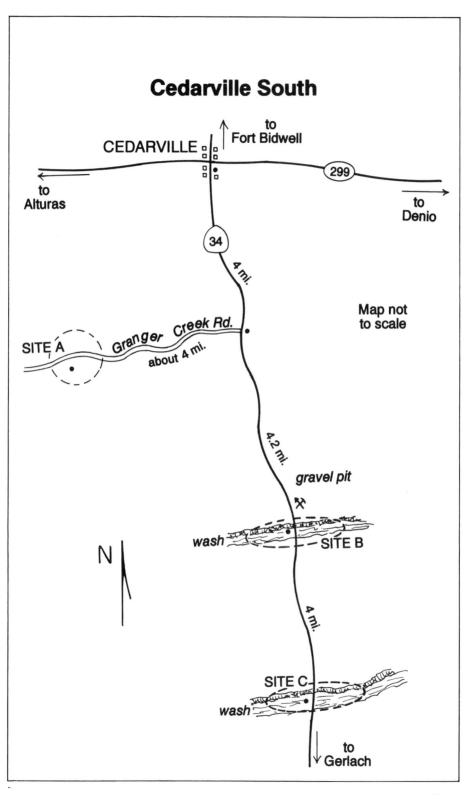

Cedarville South

CEDARVILLE

to Fort Bidwell

to Alturas

299

to Denio

34

4 mi.

Granger Creek Rd.

SITE A

about 4 mi.

Map not to scale

4.2 mi.

gravel pit

wash

SITE B

N

4 mi.

SITE C

wash

to Gerlach

41

CEDARVILLE WOOD AND AGATE

At Site "A" look for agate and occasional chunks of petrified wood on both sides of the ruts leading up the hill north of the main road. Pine needles cover most of the ground, so a small rake might be useful for exposing underlying rocks. The agate is generally white or clear, with some containing nice bands. Most has an orange crust, however, so any suspicious stones should be split to determine their true identity. Unusual, contorted chunks of agate can also be found here, and these make fascinating display pieces without being polished. Four-wheel drive vehicles can negotiate the road leading up the hill, but it is more productive to walk. Nothing is overly concentrated and most of what can be found is quite small. Be patient, though, and you should find worthwhile quantities in a relatively short amount of time.

The road to Site "B" is washed out at Cedar Creek, but occasional chunks of agate and petrified wood are available north of the waterway. The best, however, is obtained by walking a little less than one-half mile along what remains of the road on the south side of the creek. If you choose to take that hike, be very careful when fording across the water since its depth can be deceiving. If you do not feel it is safe to cross, be satisfied with what can be found on the hillsides between the highway and the creek. If you are patient and willing to take some time to exlpore the area, you will be able to gather acceptable amounts of agate and wood.

Cedarville Wood

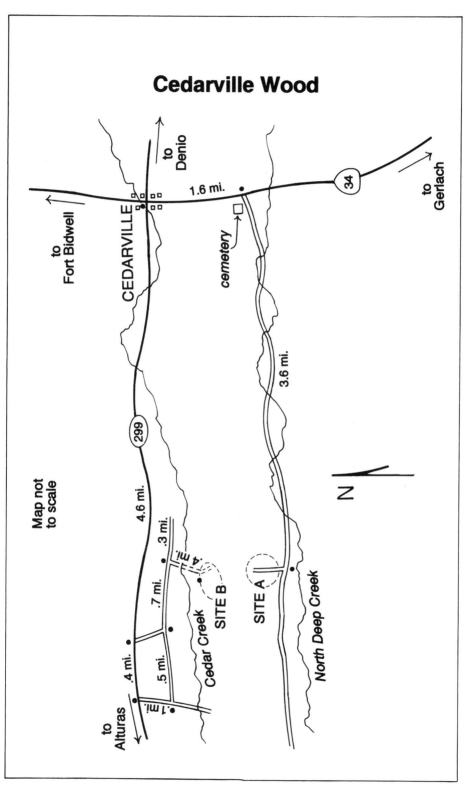

DAVIS CREEK

This location is situated in California, not far from the Nevada border, and is one of the best places in the country to find gem grade obsidian. Since so much can be found on the surface, you probably won't need heavy digging tools, however, while working at these sites, always keep in mind that obsidian is volcanic glass and shatters easily. Collectors are advised to wear gloves and goggles, especially if they plan to split any boulders.

Site "A" is extensive, consisting of acres of obsidian-covered flatlands. Most is black, but some is a pleasing brown color. The quality and size varies considerably, with most of the gem material being somewhat small. Site "B" is similar to Site "A", but the terrain is more mountainous and tree covered. There also seems to be a greater amount of gem material available there. The site is centered around the intersection shown on the map, and continues for quite a distance in all directions.

Site "C" is famous obsidian needle hill, probably the best known of these localities. Glassy needles cover the mountain and it takes minimal effort to gather hundreds of them in a very short amount of time. In addition, one can find large chunks of obsidian, including beautiful double flow brown and black pieces that display fascinating spotted and swirled patterns. Most of what can be found here is top quality and the quantity is unbelievable. At Site "D", you must hike up a steep trail to the main digging area where rainbow obsidian can be obtained. Site "E" boasts more obsidian, including a nice iris variety.

Collecting obsidian at Site "B"

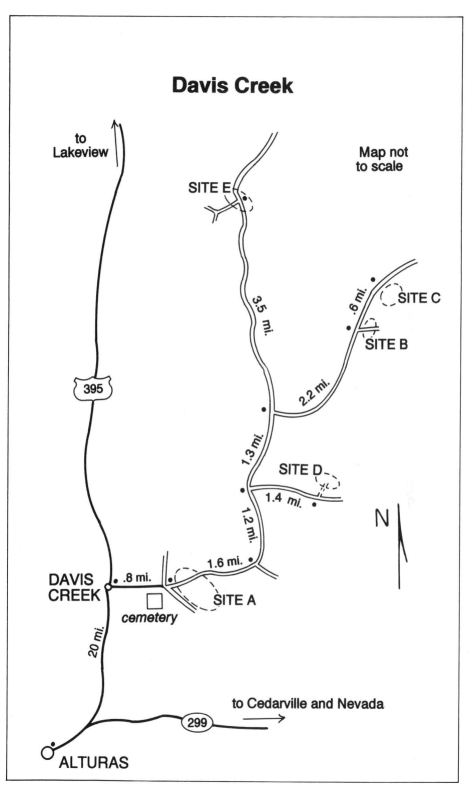

Davis Creek

to
Lakeview

Map not
to scale

SITE E

3.5 mi.

.6 mi.

SITE C

SITE B

2.2 mi.

395

1.3 mi.

SITE D

1.4 mi.

1.2 mi.

N

1.6 mi.

DAVIS
CREEK

.8 mi.

cemetery

SITE A

20 mi.

to Cedarville and Nevada

299

ALTURAS

45

NELLIE SPRING OPALITE

This location boasts outstanding specimens of opalite, occurring in a wide range of colors, frequently filled with unusual and interesting inclusions. As is the case with most opalite, much of what can be found here is substantially fractured, but it doesn't take much effort to gather a quantity of good solid material in a short amount of time.

Best access to this remote location is from Cedarville, California, as shown on the map. Go east on Highway 299 for nineteen and one-half miles. The pavement ends shortly after leaving town, but the road is well maintained and should present no problems to rugged vehicles, as long as the road is driven carefully. At the given mileage, turn south and proceed toward Gerlach, twenty and one-tenths miles, to where a large cattle pen will be encountered on the left. Just beyond, is a road with a Bureau of Land Management sign designating it to be the route to Nellie Spring. Go east four and eight-tenths miles, then right, around the small dam, six-tenths of a mile, and across the wash another one and four-tenths miles to where some ruts intersect on the right.

Follow those ruts about three-tenths of a mile, and then on the left, you will see pits that are the opalite diggings. Another similar deposit is situated about six-tenths of a mile further east, as shown. The best collecting is in and around the excavations, but additional material can be scattered throughout much of the surrounding terrain.

The opalite tends to display a good range of pleasing pastel colors, including cream, yellow, orange and brown. If you want to remove specimens directly from the deposit, be sure to wear goggles and gloves, since it splinters easily when struck with a hammer.

Be sure, while here, to explore the hills to the south. There, you can often find more opalite, occasional pieces of petrified wood, jasper, obsidian, and even arrowheads and ancient Indian chippings, all helping to make this a most productive and interesting location to visit.

Gathering opalite at the prime digging area

Nellie Spring

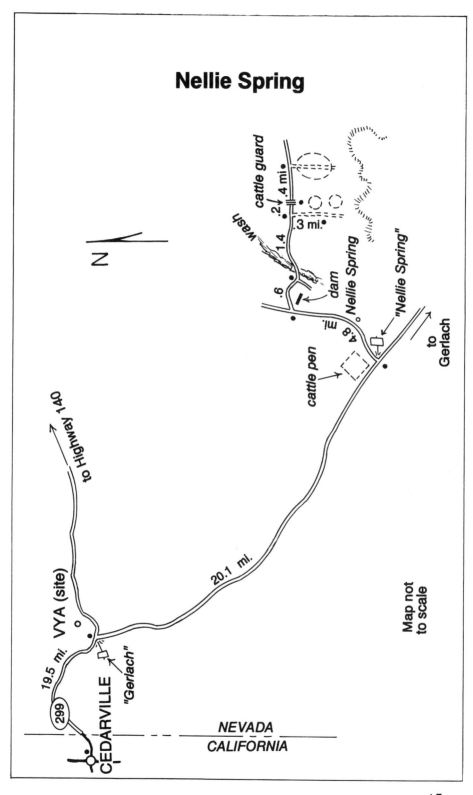

cattle guard

.2 .4 mi.

.3 mi.

wash

1.4

.6

dam

Nellie Spring

.8 mi.

"Nellie Spring"

to Gerlach

cattle pen

N

to Highway 140

VYA (site)

20.1 ml.

Map not to scale

19.5 ml.

299

CEDARVILLE

"Gerlach"

NEVADA
CALIFORNIA

Garnet-Garnet Hill

Geodes and nodules-Rabbit Springs

Texas Spring limb casts

Specimen found at Bogwood Diggings

Opalite-Nellie Springs

Apache tears and obsidian-Big Springs

Collectibles found in Vya to Gerlach area

*Agate nodules, opal and petrified wood
Trinity Mountains*

VYA TO GERLACH MINERALS

The isolated road connecting the ruins of Vya with the town of Gerlach offers rockhounds a scenic setting within which to pursue their hobby. Best access to these sites is from Cedarville, California, as shown on the map. From town, go east nineteen and one-half miles and then turn south onto the Gerlach Road, and drive about 26 miles to the northern edge of Site "A". This location boasts an unlimited quantity of nice, often gem quality, Apache tears. They are scattered all over the road and surrounding terrain, a field that extends at least another two miles south. Stop anywhere within that stretch and gather as many of the little gemstones as you desire.

Site "B" is easily spotted one and eight-tenths miles south of the northern edge of Site "A", and consists of a series of badlands-like hills, on the right. Scattered throughout those hills and adjacent terrain is lots of obsidian, colorful opalite and small pieces of petrified wood. This is a fun place to explore and you shouldn't hesitate to inspect any of the nearby similar geological formations, since most offer additional collecting opportunities.

From Site "B" continue south another two and six-tenths miles to where a road intersects from the west, that marking the center of Site "C". There you will be able to pick up additional Apache tears, obsidian, opalite, chalcedony, jasper and petrified wood. Good specimens of bubbly psilomelane have also been found there. One and eight-tenths mile further south the road to Grass Valley intersects, and at that intersection collectors can procure more obsidian, Apache tears, agate, opalite, and petrified wood, most of which is relatively small, but frequently colorful.

In continuing to Gerlach, about 34 more miles, you will go through some spectacular canyons, and the trip is highly recommended.

View of the hill in the center of Site "D"

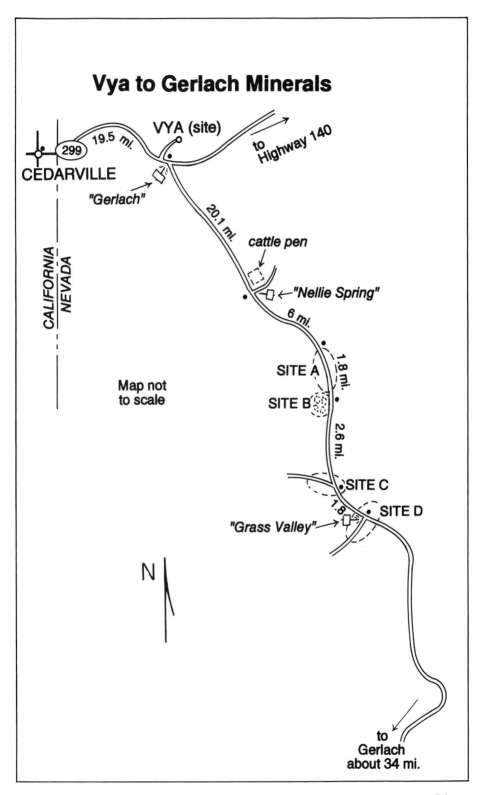

Vya to Gerlach Minerals

VYA (site)

to Highway 140

299   19.5 mi.

CEDARVILLE

"Gerlach"

CALIFORNIA | NEVADA

20.1 mi.

cattle pen

←"Nellie Spring"

6 mi.

Map not
to scale

SITE A

1.8 mi.

SITE B

2.6 mi.

SITE C

1.8

"Grass Valley"→

SITE D

N

to
Gerlach
about 34 mi.

BLACK ROCK PRECIOUS OPAL

At time of publication, this site was temporarily closed, and is mentioned here in hopes that it will soon be reopened. The Black Rock Opal Mine boasts an opportunity for collectors to gather beautiful specimens of fire-filled precious opal. At one time the prospect was known as the Little Joe, but the name was changed when ownership was transferred in 1984. The current owner, Mr. David Pooley, is attempting to interest investors in purchasing badly needed heavy equipment to clear overburden and thereby expose the opal bearing ground.

The opal occurs in the rough, dark gray andesite and basalt. It is generally a clear jelly type, with occasional pieces being milky white. The internal "fire" encompasses the entire spectrum, with brilliant red and green seeming to predominate. It is strenuous work removing the tough volcanic host rock from its place in the hillside, and even more difficult to extract the opal without damaging it. Rockhounds should have hard rock tools, goggles, gloves, plenty of energy and lots of patience. Be sure to also take some supplies, since you will be many dusty miles from the nearest town.

Agates, geodes and jasper can also be gathered in the territory surrounding the mine, as can an occasional arrowhead and even petrified wood.

To determine the current status of the Black Rock Opal Mine, write to David Pooley, P.O. Box 149, Gerlach, Nevada 89412. Do not visit the mine without prior approval. You will find Mr. Pooley most congenial and helpful, and it is hoped he can find the financial assistance he needs to reopen this most significant Nevada collecting site.

Black Rock Precious Opal

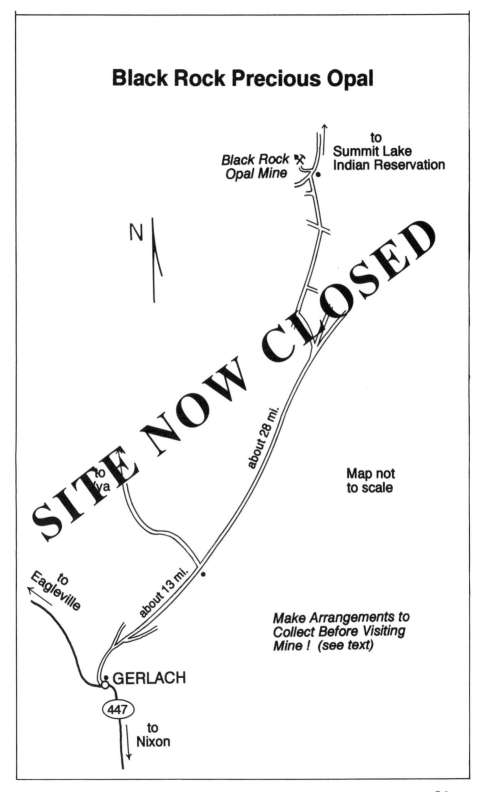

Black Rock
Opal Mine

to
Summit Lake
Indian Reservation

N

about 28 mi.

to
~ya

Map not
to scale

to
Eagleville

about 13 mi.

Make Arrangements to
Collect Before Visiting
Mine ! (see text)

GERLACH

447

to
Nixon

SITE NOW CLOSED

TRINITY MOUNTAINS AGATE

This interesting trip provides rockhounds an opportunity to gather unusual and often colorful agate nodules, opal and petrified wood. The road isn't too bad, but the trip should only be attempted in rugged vehicles since you must traverse some rocky areas. To get to Summit Peak, the center of the collecting area, start in Lovelock and take Western Avenue two and six-tenths mile west from town as illustrated on the map. At that point, bear straight ahead, another one-half mile. Go left, through the dump area, eleven and one-tenth miles, and then climb into the hills by bearing right at the fork one and seven-tenths mile. From there, just before heading down a steep hill, ruts will be seen leading off to the right toward Summit Peak, about one-half mile away. Follow those tracks to the base of the rhyolite pinnacle. That is the center of the collecting area.

Common opal is often found in the unusual rhyolite bubbles that occur throughout the base of the hill. There are also reports of precious opal having been found here, even though specimens of that prized mineral are very rare. The agate tends to be scattered, in sometimes sizable chunks, about the hillsides and lower areas. Just spend time roaming the landscape and doing some scrambling on the rocky regions at the base of the peak and you should be able to obtain lots of fine material in a short amount of time.

Specimens of rhyolite which are covered with the unusual bubbles make interesting display pieces, as they are. The nodules range in diameter from less than an inch to some measuring larger than a baseball. The opal is found in many pastel colors, primarily light green, yellow and white. The agate tends to display plume-like patterns, in shades of orange, red, yellow, green, brown, white, and purple.

A view of Summit Peak at the center of the collecting area

Trinity Mountains

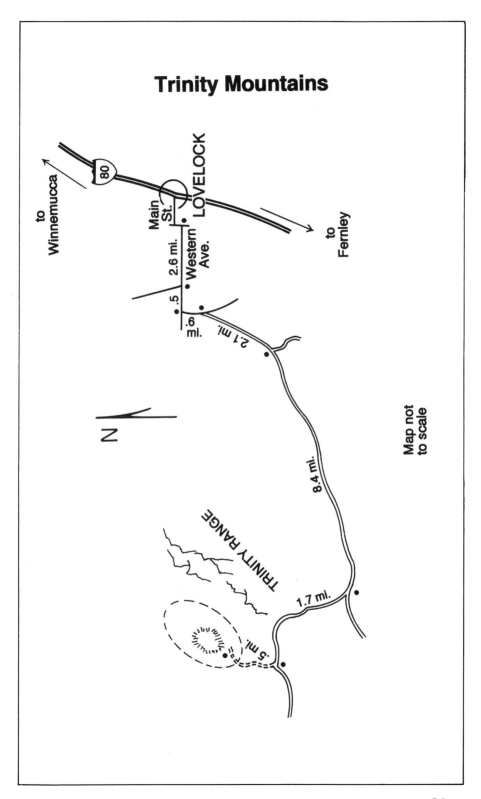

LOVELOCK AGATE

Opalite, agate and petrified wood can be gathered throughout the mountainous terrain northwest of Lovelock. To get there, go north from town on Highway 398 about one and one-half miles to Highway 399, and then proceed left for about 10 more miles to where a sign designates the the turn to the Seven Troughs Sulphur Mine. Stay on the pavement as it bears left at that point another five miles. At the given mileage, there is a sign designating the beginning of the Eagle Picher Mine property. Their land extends along the roadway another one and two-tenths miles. Under no circumstances, should rockhounds violate the rights of the claim holders and procure minerals there.

Just two-tenths of a mile past the last Eagle Picher Mine sign, ruts will be seen heading off to the left, and it is there that you should park. Search throughout the hills to the north of the main road where extremely colorful agate and petrified wood can be found. The wood tends to be brown and gray, and the agate can be found in a variety of colors, often filled with fascinating inclusions. The prize hue, however, is a brilliant red variety which polishes beautifully. Just park and hike as far as you like, being careful not to loose your bearings.

If you follow the ruts to the south a few tenths of a mile, more agate and petrified wood can be found in the hills to the east, and a producitve opalite area occurs just west of the road. The opalite diggings are not too difficult to spot. Simply look for scars in the landscape as indications of where previous rockhounds have dug.

There is a good place to set up camp just north of the main road where the ruts lead off to the south. There is so much to find here, and the collecting area extends for such a distance, that it might be worthwhile to spend a few days.

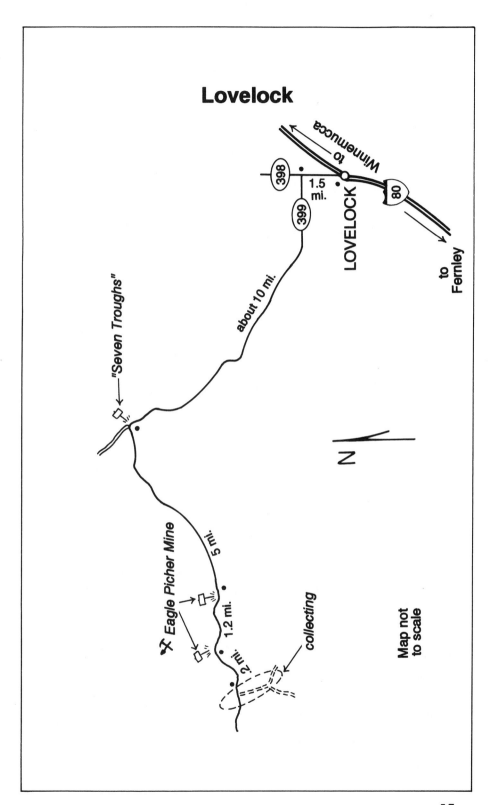

Lovelock

to Winnemucca

to Fernley

LOVELOCK

80

398

399

1.5 mi.

about 10 mi.

"Seven Troughs"

N

Eagle Picher Mine

5 mi.

1.2 mi.

.2 mi.

collecting

Map not to scale

FERNLEY AGATE

A variety of generally colorful agate can be found scattered randomly throughout the countryside south of Fernley. To get to this easily accessible site from town, head south on Highway 95A about five miles to the city dump turnoff. From that point, scattered on both sides of the highway, the hills provide rockhounds with lots of agate, some of a very high quality. There are no overwhelming concentrations of material anywhere, so it does take some patient hiking and searching to find worthwhile quantities. However, the locale provides a serene and pleasant place to conduct your exploration.

The most accessible portion of this vast area is reached by continuing south on Highway 95A eight-tenths of a mile past the dump turnoff to where ruts can be seen leading off to the right. Follow them two-tenths of a mile to where another road is encountered. Go either direction on that intersecting road, park, and hike west, looking carefully for the agate as you go.

If you don't have much luck at your first stop, drive a little further and try again. Some of the agate, especially that which is in the flatlands, tends to be covered with a brown film due to the dusty native soil, thereby making identification sometimes difficult. For that reason, this location is most productive immediately after a cleansing rainstorm, if you can endure the sticky mud. The agate is found in a wide range of colors, with a multitude of internal patterns and inclusions. Some is rather colorless, but others are beautiful, filled with moss and dendrites, and capable of producing fantastic polished pieces.

Gathering agate at the collecting site

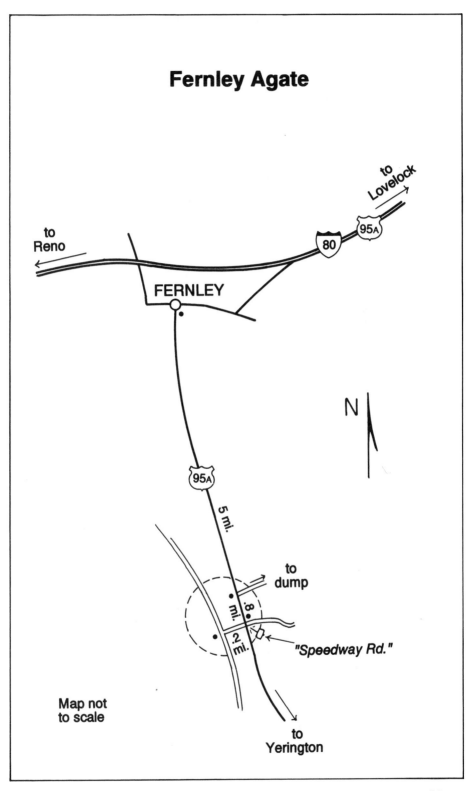

Fernley Agate

to Lovelock

95A

80

to Reno

FERNLEY

N

95A

5 mi.

to dump

.8 mi.

.2 mi.

"Speedway Rd."

to Yerington

Map not
to scale

LAKE LAHONTAN AGATE

Although rockhounding is not allowed within the boundaries of Lake Lahontan State Recreation Area, lots of fine cutting materials can be procured just outside its boundaries. The best collecting seems to be north of Highway 50, on either side of the railroad tracks. Simply park in any convenient spot,well off the pavement, and hike through the low hills searching for chert, agate, petrified wood and jasper, some of which is very colorful. Ocassionally, the agate displays vivid red and black inclusions, and such material can be used to produce exquisite polished items. It seems that the best concentrations are centered around the railroad track, and hiking further to the north will generally not lend to better hunting.

The agate, jasper, chert and petrified wood are scattered over a wide area, and high quality material is not overly plentiful. Most of what is found here is relatively small, but fine tumbling material can be gathered with little effort. In spite of the site's shortcomings it does offer a great place to camp next to beautiful Lake Lahontan. At time of publication, camping was permitted anywhere alongside the water except in designated recreation areas.

There are over 70 miles of shoreline along the lake, and the fishing is good. In addition, there are picnic grounds with restroom facilites and two campgrounds, but with no hookups. All of these facilities, in addition to the cool lake in which to soak your weary feet, make this a great place to stop for a few hours or an evening, on a rockhounding journey through Nevada.

Collecting just <u>outside the boundaries</u> of Lake Lahontan State Park

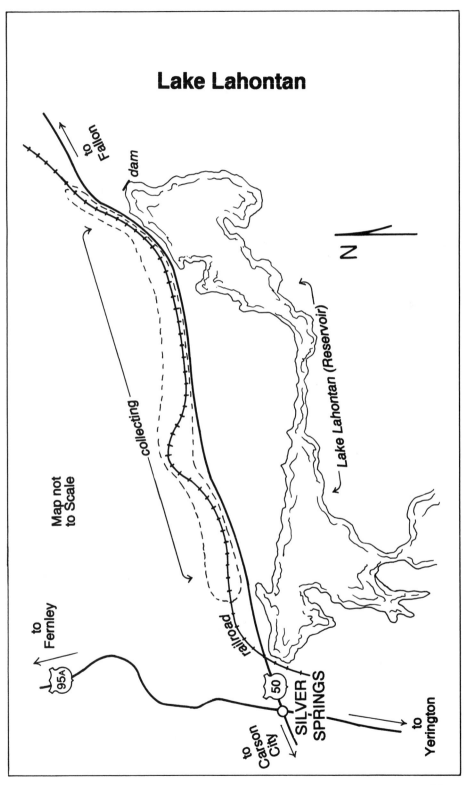

Lake Lahontan

to Fallon

dam

Map not
to Scale

to Fernley

95A

collecting

railroad

Lake Lahontan (Reservoir)

N

50

SILVER
SPRINGS

to Carson City

to Yerington

61

SILVER SPRINGS SELENITE

Agate, jasper and lots of fine selenite can be gathered in the mining region south of Silver Springs. To get there, take Highway 95A south from town 11 miles, and then turn west onto the ruts another seven-tenths of a mile. Be sure to close the gate after passing through. At the given mileage you will be in the center of an extensive abandoned mine, and it is there that you should park. If the mine appears to no longer be abandoned when you visit, restrict collecting to outside its boundaries. Be also advised that there are numerous claim markers on the surrounding hills, and it would be best to restrict your collecting to regions outside those areas also, even though most appear to be out of date and abandoned.

The agate and jasper can be found scattered throughout the region. Some is very colorful, but both tend to be scarce and small. It is great for tumbling and fairly easy to spot due to its vivid coloration against the lighter colored soil. The selenite can be found "growing" out of the soft gray soil of the unusual mounds in and around the mine. Some is merely a thin crust on the surface, while other is much thicker, frequently exhibiting the fibrous crystal structure indigenous of that mineral. Careful digging in the mounds will sometimes unearth larger pieces, but generally the most productive way of gathering the interesting, semi-transparent gypsum ore is to carefully scrutinize the surface. Remember that selenite is very fragile, and specimens should be well protected for the journey home.

Don't hesitate to do a little walking in the hills, since the agate and jasper is widely scattered. If you do hike, though, be careful not to loose your bearings.

Looking for selenite crystals in the gray hills

Silver Springs Selenite

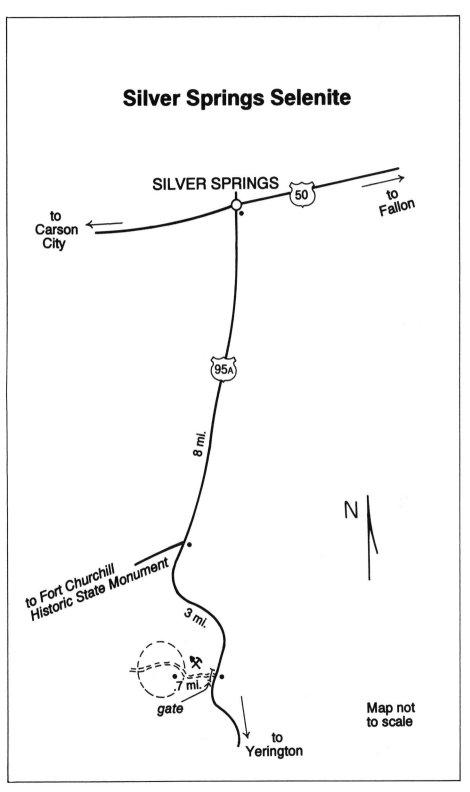

SILVER SPRINGS

50

to
Fallon

to
Carson
City

95A

8 mi.

N

to Fort Churchill
Historic State Monument

3 mi.

.7 mi.

gate

Map not
to scale

to
Yerington

WONDERSTONE MOUNTAIN

Top quality specimens of the swirled and colorful variety of rhyolite known as wonderstone can be found only a short distance southeast of Fallon, this being one of the state's premier rockhounding sites. To get there, follow Highway 50 about ten miles southeast from Fallon to a sign that designates the turnoff to Grimes Point. Go east on that fairly well graded road, bearing left at the first major fork and right at the second as illustrated on the map. After having traveled four and eight-tenths miles, you will encounter some pits and mounds on the left. Just before reaching those pits, tracks lead off to the northeast toward prominent Wonderstone Montain, only a few tenths of a mile away.

The entire mountain is composed of the interesting, swirled rhyolite, but much is somewhat pourous, thereby not capable of taking a good polish. In addition, some displays much better banding and patterning than others. For those reasons, be sure to allow plenty of time to fully explore the entire mountain. Look for digging pits where previous rockhounds may have found worthwhile specimens, since such locations should provide good indicators as to where you should commence your search. Lots of specimens can be found scattered all over the ground, especially near the numerous digging pits, but such surface material is generally quite small. If you want larger or better pieces, it is usually necessary to employ hard rock tools such as gads, chisels and pry bars to remove the tough rhyolite from its place in the mountain.

Be sure to take insect repellent since it seems mosquitos and gnats also like Wonderstone Mountain.

Working in a pit on Wonderstone Mountain

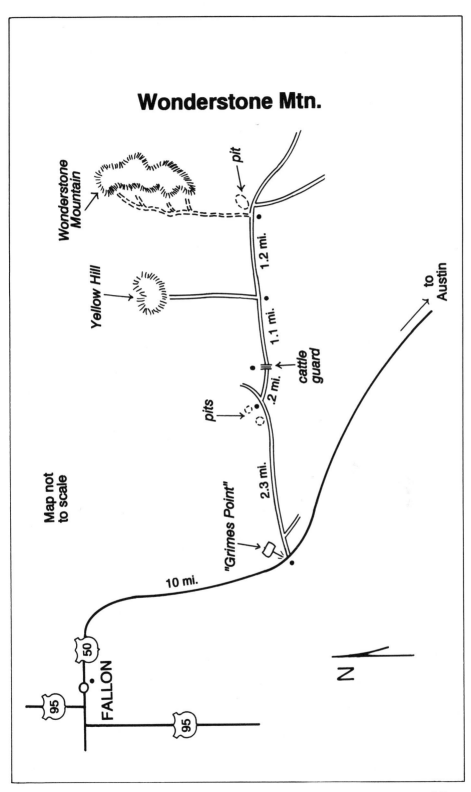

Wonderstone Mtn.

pit

Wonderstone Mountain

Yellow Hill

1.2 mi.

1.1 mi.

cattle guard

.2 mi.

pits

2.3 mi.

to Austin

Map not to scale

"Grimes Point"

10 mi.

50

FALLON

95

95

N

65

GREEN MOUNTAIN AGATE

Green Mountain is situated only a short distance from Fallon in the same general area as Wonderstone Mountain. To get there, take Highway 50 southeast from town about ten miles to where a sign designates the turnoff to Grimes Point. Follow the mileage provided on the map to the tracks leading up the wash labeled as Site "A". If your vehicle can traverse deep sand, proceed into the wash about seven-tenths of a mile. Otherwise, park and hike. This is a fairly extensive site, and encompasses the wash and much of the surrounding terrain on either side. Lots of agate and wonderstone can be found in float, but the finest of the agate is procured by using hard rock tools to extract it from veins situated in the hills about 50 feet west of the wash.

Green Mountain, designated as Site "B" on the map, is an easy to spot landmark, and boasts a wide variety of desirable collectables around its circumference. More than one road leads to Green Mountain, and it really doesn't make any difference which one you chose since minerals of interest can be found just about anywhere around the mountain. Simply park as close to the rocky base as possible and follow any of the numerous perimeter trails.

Beautiful blue lace agate, colorful jasper, and wonderstone can be found scattered throughout the softer soil surrounding the mountain, below the rocky outcrops, but the best of the lace agate is obtained by digging. In addition, Green Mountain offers a nice, green, jade-like stone, much of which will take an acceptable polish. The quality of the green rock varies greatly, though, so be certain you look only for that with the least porosity and best color.

A view of Site "A"

66

Green Mountain

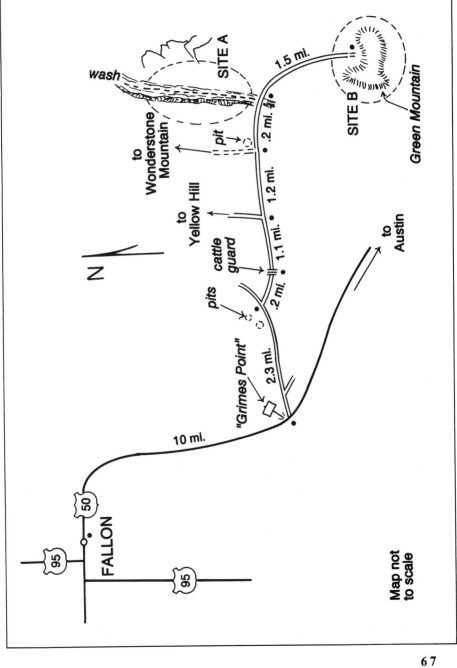

BELL CANYON AGATE

The two sites pinpointed on the accompanying map provide collectors with a variety of minerals and an opportunity to explore a remote and interesting part of Nevada's back country. To get there from Fallon, go east on Highway 50 about 32 miles to Highway 839. Turn south and proceed another seven miles to where some tracks will be seen heading off to the east. Follow those tracks about three miles to the center of Site "A".

Walk the hills and washes, keeping your eyes peeled for colorful jasper, wonderstone, bubbly chalcedony and a number of other interesting minerals. The road to Site "A" is not too bad, but it deteriorates quickly as you proceed to Site "B". Be sure your vehicle is capable of traveling in loose sand before continuing since this is a most remote region and not a place you want to get stuck.

If you choose to proceed to Site "B", go about six-tenths of a mile further east and enter the sandy wash. Follow that wash three and one-tenth miles to a gate, stopping from time to time to search for additional minerals. Go through the gate, closing it after having passed through, and continue another six-tenths of a mile to the prominent twin peaks. Park near the peaks and roam the countryside towards the hills in the north, looking for banded opalite, agate, jasper and swirled rhyolite. Much of this is very colorful, but generally not too large. Pay particularly close attention to regions of erosion. The opalite and agate tend to stand out vividly against the dark native soil, helping make the search a little easier.

You may want to explore the cliffs to the north in hopes of finding the agate and opalite bearing seams. Crystal filled geodes have also been reported as being obtained in the general locality, so be on the lookout.

Nothing seems to be overly concentrated in any particular spot at either site, so it is necessary to exhibit patience, persistence and a willingness to do some walking. The quality tends to be very good, however, helping to make that extra effort worthwhile.

The twin peaks marking the center of Site "B"

Bell Canyon

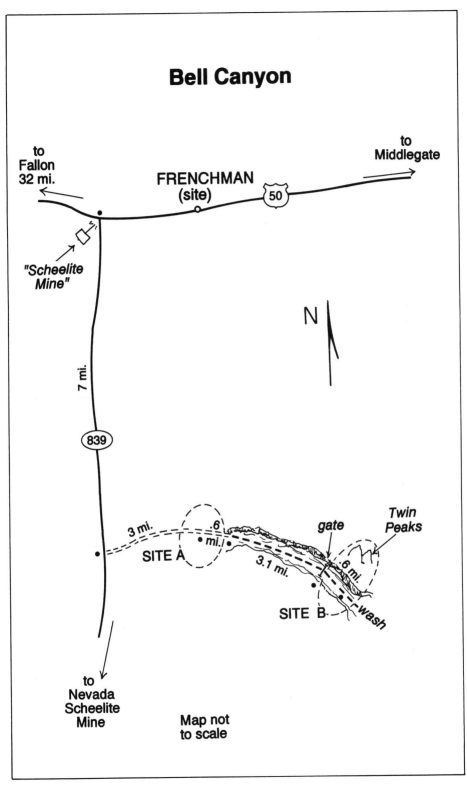

to
Fallon
32 mi.

FRENCHMAN
(site)

50

to
Middlegate

"Scheelite
Mine"

7 mi.

839

N

3 mi.

.6
mi.

SITE A

gate

Twin
Peaks

3.1 mi.

.6 mi.

SITE B

wash

to
Nevada
Scheelite
Mine

Map not
to scale

MIDDLE GATE GEODES, JASPER AND AGATE

Crystal filled geodes, chalcedony, colorful jasper and agate are just some of the minerals to be found at the two sites illustrated on the accompanying map. To get to this somewhat remote, but highly productive collecting locality, go east from Fallon 32 miles to Highway 839 where there is a sign indicating the road to the Nevada Scheelite Mine. Proceed south eight and nine-tenths miles and then follow the tracks leading east seven-tenths of a mile further. At that point, turn right and continue another three and nine-tenths miles, then left, up the arroyo, about two tenths of a mile to Site "A". If your vehicle cannot travel through loose sand, park and hike that final short distance.

Collecting continues at least one-half mile further, and lots of colorful jasper, agate, chalcedony, and tiny crystal filled nodules can be found scattered throughout the wash and surrounding countryside.

To reach Site "B" return to the main road, go another four-tenths of a mile, and then turn left into the wash. Proceed another one-half mile if (and only if) your vehicle is capable of traveling in deep sand. To your left at the given mileage, just the other side of the shallow hills, there is some picturesque badlands scenery. Within the wash, surrounding countryside and throughout the badlands, collectors can find crystal filled geodes and multicolored jasper. In addition, there is chalcedony and agate, some of which is filled with interesting inclusions.

If you have the time and the energy, be sure to explore the hills separating Site "A" and Site "B", since that region also offers additional collecting opportunities.

Parked at Site "B"

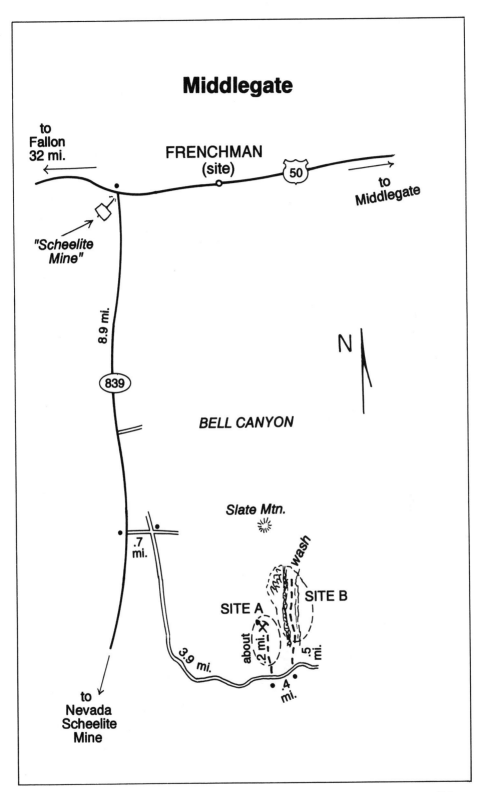

Middlegate

to
Fallon
32 mi.

FRENCHMAN
(site)

50

to
Middlegate

"Scheelite
Mine"

8.9 mi.

839

N

BELL CANYON

Slate Mtn.

.7
mi.

wash

SITE A

SITE B

about
.2 mi.

3.9 mi.

.5
mi.

.4
mi.

to
Nevada
Scheelite
Mine

BUFFALO CANYON FOSSILS

Interesting fossilized remnants of trees and other plant life that inhabited central Nevada about ten million years ago can be obtained in the numerous shale deposits of Buffalo Canyon. To get to this scenic locality, go east from Middle Gate on Highway 50 about three miles and then bear right onto Highway 722. Continue seven and five-tenths miles. Where you leave the pavement go straight ahead another four and nine-tenths miles. The final stretch of road is generally well-maintained and should present no difficulty to rugged vehicles. At the given mileage, turn left and follow the tracks only about one-tenth of a mile, pull to the side, and hike up the colorful mounds on the left to any of the shale ridges.

It is within the shale that collectors can find nice leaf fossils and imprints, the most common of which are ancient descendants of the contemporary oak tree. In addition, sycamore, ash, willow and elm leaves can be obtained, as well as juniper twigs, seeds and reeds. The best are procured by carefully splitting the thin, bluish shale situated about half way up the hillsides, but fine examples can also be discovered in just about all other layers. Just be patient and careful when separating the shale. Be sure to use the proper tools and exhibit patience when removing the encasing rock so no damage is done to the delicate fossils. Pieces containing many leaves are outstanding for display.

If you have time, be sure to exlpore some of the other shale outcrops in the region, since they, too, provide good fossil finding potential.

In the lowlands, rockhounds can pick up opalite, agate and jasper, but it is not overly plentiful and generally tends to be small.

Colorful common opal has been unearthed in regions of contact between diatomite and volcanic rock further up Buffalo Canyon. To get there, bear right at the fork and proceed about one mile to the old diamite open pit mine. From there, continuing on the left at least another one-half mile, the opal can be found in vivid shades of red, purple, brown and white. Most, however, is very fractured, and it takes some patient searching to gather chunks clean enough for polishing.

A general view of the collecting area

Buffalo Canyon

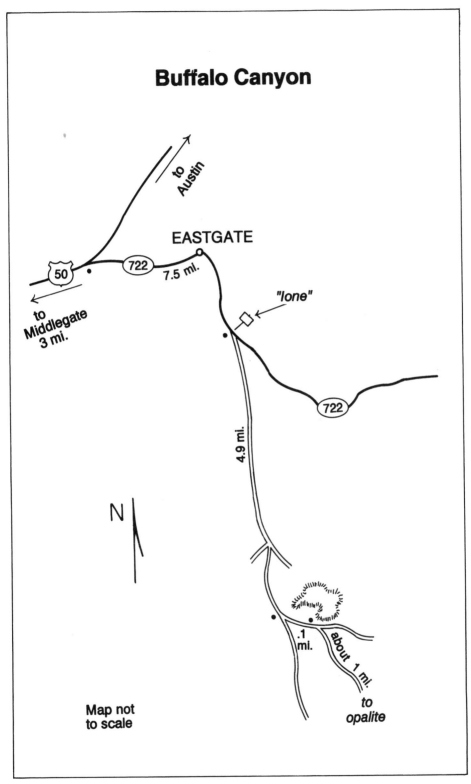

to Austin

EASTGATE

50   722   7.5 mi.

to Middlegate 3 mi.

"Ione"

722

4.9 mi.

N

.1 mi.

about 1 mi.

to opalite

Map not to scale

QUARTZ MOUNTAIN MINERALS &
PETRIFIED WOOD

Quartz crystals, pyrite, galena and petrified wood all can be found in an extensive region between Highway 361 and the Quartz Mountain Mine, a short distance north of Gabbs. To get to this interesting locality, go north from town 14 miles to where a sign designates the turnoff to Broken Hills and Quartz Mountain. Proceed east on the graded dirt road only a short distance, pull off and park. Petrified wood can be found randomly scattered thorughout the hills on either side of the road for quite a distance, as can occasional colorful chunks of agate and jasper. Nothing is overly plentiful, though, and it takes some patient and dedicated searching to find much. Two miles in from the highway is the Broken Hills Mine. Trespassing is not allowed there, but some mineral specimens can be found in the non-posted dumps immediately adjacent to the road.

The best chance for finding pyrite, galena and tiny quartz filled vugs is at the Quartz Mountain Mine, another two and two-tenths miles along the road bearing right at the fork, as shown on the map. At time of publication, this prospect was abandoned, and dump collecting was not restricted. Do not, however, even consider entering any of the tunnels, since they are very unstable. If the collecting status has changed, be sure to affirm your right to collect there before doing so.

The Quartz Mountain Mine not only offers rockhounds a great place to gather minerals, but also provides a number of great photo opportunities.

A portion of the Quartz Mountain dumps

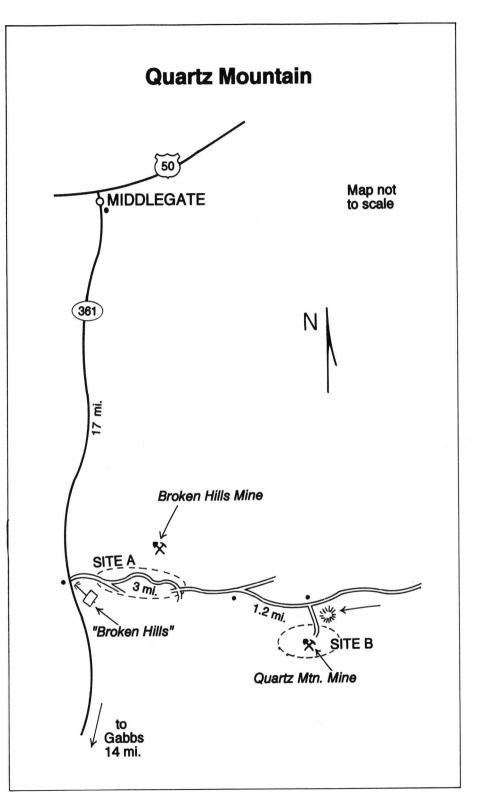

Quartz Mountain

50

○ MIDDLEGATE
●

Map not
to scale

361

N

17 mi.

Broken Hills Mine

SITE A

3 mi.

"Broken Hills"

1.2 mi.

SITE B

Quartz Mtn. Mine

to
Gabbs
14 mi.

MONTE CRISTO JASPER

A huge field of jasper, agate and petrified wood is situated only 13 miles north of Gabbs, just off Highway 361. To get there, go three-tenths of a mile north of the Mineral County/Nye County boundary line and turn west towards the hills. Proceed about one-half mile, park to the side, and start walking. There is lots of colorful jasper and it isn't difficult to spot due to its bright, clean color which stands out brilliantly against the native soil. Some is multi-colored, while others are a single hue. Most is solid, but occasional chunks do contain pits or porous regions.

The agate is not as plentiful, but still worth looking for. It primarily occurs in the form of interesting nodules and such specimens are great for tumbling, often producing extremely interesting results. Most of the agate is clear, but some contains intricate inclusions and/or patterns of differing colors, those being the most prized. The petrified wood tends to be rather plain, primarily in shades of gray and brown, but some contains regions of orange or red, making them desirable for polishing. The wood tends to be small but larger samples are available. Such pieces are great for display, as is, since they usually exhibit their ancient exterior wood structure very well.

As mentioned earlier, this is an extensive collecting field; it is highly recommended that you continue west along the road toward the mountains for at least another two miles, stopping as many times as you desire. The jasper, agate and wood tend to be randomly dispersed, so, if you have limited success at one stop, drive a little further and try again. Be certain, as you hike, not to loose your bearings. It is a good idea to walk a distance from the road, since this is a well known collecting site, but it can be traumatic if you can't find your car when ready to return.

Collecting at the site

Monte Cristo Jasper

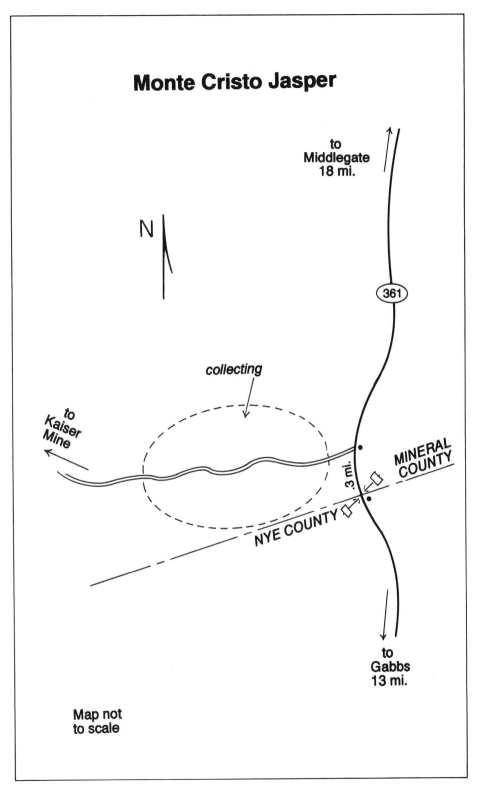

to
Middlegate
18 mi.

N

361

collecting

to
Kaiser
Mine

MINERAL
COUNTY

.3 mi.

NYE COUNTY

to
Gabbs
13 mi.

Map not
to scale

GABBS OPALIZED WOOD

This somewhat remote collecting area boasts fine samples of opalized wood, petrified wood, agate, jasper, chalcedony, Apache tears and pink feldspar. To get to the primary location, take Highway 361 north from Gabbs two and nine-tenths miles, and then follow the graded road on the left, nine and nine-tenths miles, being certain to remain on the main thoroughfare as it winds its way westward. At the given mileage, there is a fork where you should bear right another one-tenth of a mile and then go right again, continuing two miles to the edge of a wash where you should park. It is important to note that good specimens of agate, jasper, wood and Apache tears can be found, randomly, all along the road to the collecting site. It is usually worth the effort to stop a few times and do some exploring.

The primary collecting is centered around the grayish hills, about one-fourth of a mile from the road, as illustrated on the map. The hills can be seen as you approach, thereby not being difficult to find. The terrain around the parking area and all the way to the mounds, provides great potential for finding minerals of interest. Nothing is highly concentrated, so it takes some patient searching to gather good quantities. However, lots can be picked up in a short time.

The opalized wood tends to be the most scarce, being found essentially on the southern slopes and washes of the gray hills. Most is easy to spot, due to its often bright color which stands out vividly against the native soil. Do not loose sight of where you park your vehicle, since it is easy to get disoriented here. Try to park on high ground, and not in the wash or a low spot.

Specimens found at the site

Gabbs Wood

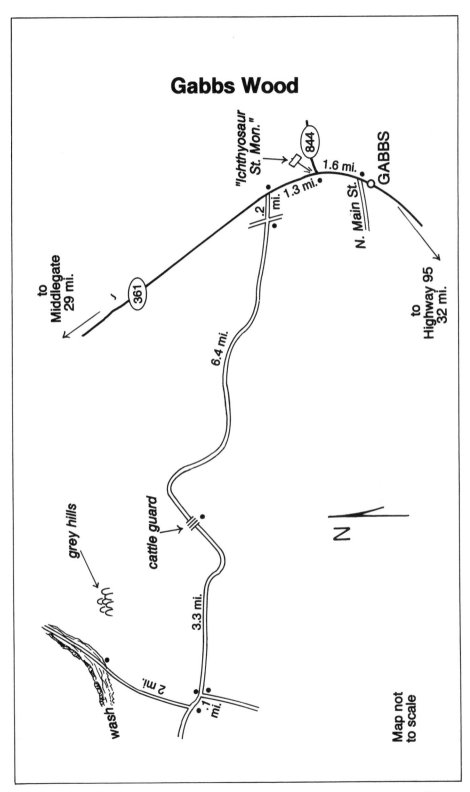

"Ichthyosaur St. Mon."

844

1.6 mi.

GABBS

.2 mi.

1.3 mi.

N. Main St.

to
Middlegate
29 mi.

361

to
Highway 95
32 mi.

6.4 mi.

grey hills

cattle guard

N

3.3 mi.

2 mi.

.1 mi.

wash

Map not
to scale

DEEP SPRINGS SMOKEY QUARTZ

This is a great place to find well formed, deep black smokey quartz crystals ranging from very small to many inches in length.

To get to this interesting site, which is situated just west of the Nevada border, either take Highway 266 southwest from Dyer or Highway 266 northwest through Lida until you come to Highway 168. From there, continue west on Highway 168 to the Deep Springs Highway maintenance station, about eleven more miles, and then another two and two-tenths miles to a cattle guard. Just after crossing the cattle guard, there are some ruts on the right paralleling a fence to the crystal bearing hill, seven-tenths of a mile from the pavement. If coming from Big Pine, California, the turnoff is twelve and four-tenths miles east of the road to Bristlecone Pine Forest.

Raking through the soil on the lower slopes will frequently expose loose crystals, but the most productive technique is to open cavities and seams found throughout the hill. To do this, it is necessary to have a pair of gloves, goggles, sledge hammer, gads, chisels and lots of energy, since it involves very hard work. Find a promising crack or "rotten" spot in the rock face and carefully commence breaking it down, hoping to open into a larger, crystal filled cavity. When you do come upon a cavity, it is important that you work carefully when widening the opening to facilitate removing the elusive crystals. Many beautiful specimens have been destroyed by impatient collectors carelessly breaking in with brute force and little forethought. Stuffing paper or sand into the voids will sometimes help, but always keep in mind that gaining access will take lots of time and energy. BE PATIENT and persistent since most cavities do contain the highly prized, jet black crystals.

Deep Springs

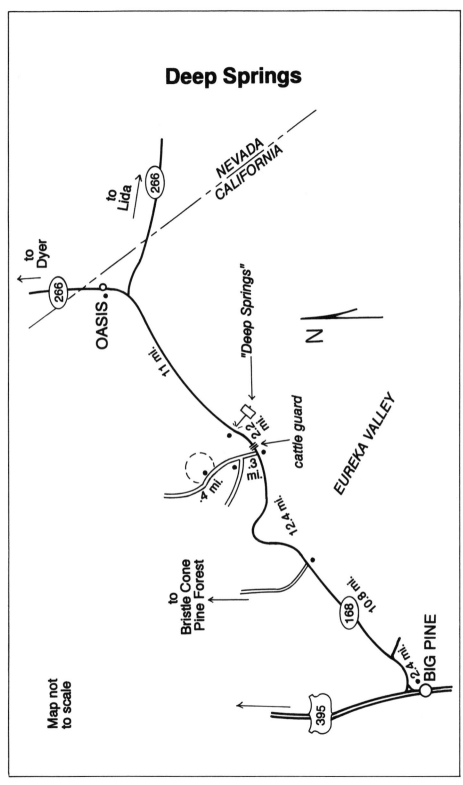

Map not to scale

to Dyer

266

to Lida

266

NEVADA
CALIFORNIA

OASIS

"Deep Springs"

N

11 mi.

.2 mi.

cattle guard

.3 mi.

.4 mi.

EUREKA VALLEY

12.4 mi.

to
Bristle Cone
Pine Forest

168

10.8 mi.

2.4 mi.

BIG PINE

395

BASALT JASPER

Colorful jasper, obsidian, petrified wood and occasional chunks of interesting agate can be found in a hidden canyon just south of Highway 6, near the site of the one-time town of Basalt. This location is accessible only in four-wheel drive, and should not be attempted with any other vehicles since it is a most inhospitable place to get stuck.

To get there, go east on Highway 6 one and seven-tenths miles from where Highway 360 intersects and follow the faint ruts heading south over the hill. Follow those tracks eight-tenths of a mile, drop into the sandy wash, turn left, proceed about three-tenths of a mile further and stop. From there exlpore the wash and surrounding hillsides as far as you want to roam, but don't loose track of where you parked.

A bridge will be encountered about two-tenths of a mile further down the arroyo. That is on the old highway which is now abandoned. Good material, some quite sizeable, can be found on the adjacent hillsides south of that crumbling stretch of pavement for quite a distance in either direction. If you choose to explore the higher regions, especially those above the wash, be very careful since the climb is steep and trecherous. The only thing worse that getting your vehicle stuck would be to become injured in such a desolate location.

The jasper is generally solid and capable of taking a good polish but some is pitted and/or porous, so be sure to gather only the best available. Colors include bright yellow and red. Occasional chunks display many hues in a variety of often pleasing patterns. The agate is more scarce, but much is filled with interesting inclusions which help to produce pleasing polished pieces. Petrified wood can also be found on some of the surrounding slopes, but it tends to be somewhat colorless and porous, consequently being suitable only for display as unpolished specimens.

Basalt Jasper

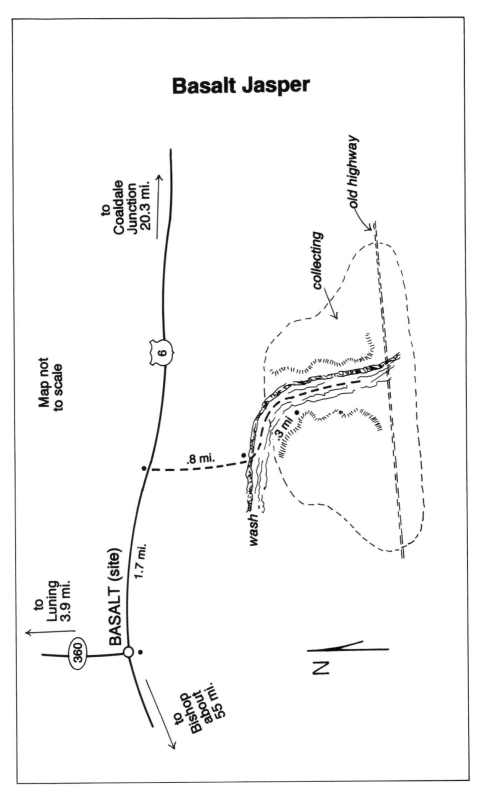

Map not
to scale

to
Coaldale
Junction
20.3 mi.

old highway

collecting

.8 mi.

.3 mi

wash

BASALT (site)

1.7 mi.

to
Luning
3.9 mi.

to
Bishop
about
55 mi.

360

6

N

THE SUMP

The area in and around the Sump, southwest of Coaldale Junction, is one of the most unusual places a rockhound can visit. Its landscape is filled with weird formations, consisting of spires of dried mud and tilted, contorted hillsides.

To get to site "A", take Highway 6 west from Coaldale Junction about six and two-tenths miles and then bear south onto Highway 264. Proceed seven and nine-tenths miles, and turn east, following the ruts leaving the pavement. Go about eight-tenths of a mile further, park, and start exploring this fascinating locality overlooking the Sump.

In addition to the spectacular view, rockhounds can gather chalcedony, opalite, agate and Apache tears on the flatlands, and, in the sandstone immediately overlooking the Sump, one can procure interesting limb and twig casts as well as petrified wood. The latter materials are found all along the the rim but are tough to spot since they are the same color as the surrounding soil. For that reason, it takes some diligent searching to locate those elusive collectibles. It is essential to be very careful here, since the sandstone is slippery and unstable. It wouldn't be tough to slip and fall quite a distance if not cautious.

To get into the Sump, continue south on Highway 264 another two miles and then turn left onto the tracks, four-tenths of a mile, to a wash. If you have four-wheel drive, enter the wash and proceed another one-half mile. Otherwise, park and hike the remaining distance.

In the Sump, one can gather petrified wood, opalite, selenite slabs, chalcedony, agate and jasper. The opalite principally occurs in seams, and some is very colorful. The wood tends to be light gray, but yellow and yellow-green chunks are not uncommon. Plan to spend some time in this most fascinating location. You will not be sorry for doing so.

A view of the Sump

The Sump

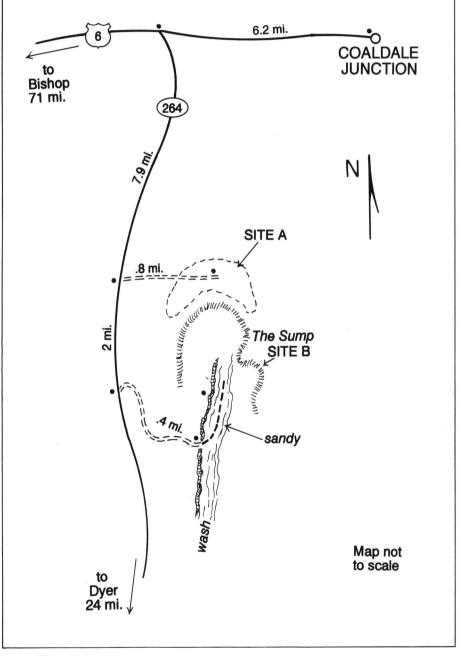

to
Bishop
71 mi.

264

6.2 mi.

COALDALE
JUNCTION

N

7.9 mi.

SITE A

.8 mi.

2 mi.

The Sump
SITE B

.4 mi.

sandy

wash

to
Dyer
24 mi.

Map not
to scale

FISH LAKE VALLEY OBSIDIAN

Fish Lake Valley offers rockhounds lots of Apache tears, some of which can be faceted for use in jewelry. To get to this scenic location from Coaldale Junction, take Highway 6 west, six and two-tenths miles, and then turn south onto Highway 264. Go only two-tenths of a mile and bear left on the dirt road branching off to the left. Continue four and seven-tenths miles to a major fork, that marks the start of the collecting area.

From the given mileage, and continuing at least five more miles southward, one can gather countless Apache tears. The concentration varies from spot to spot, but they seem to be just about everywhere. It is helpful to keep the sun behind you when looking, since such lighting normally causes the little gems to sparkle in the soil, making the search much simpler.

Size varies from quite small to those measuring up to an inch in diameter. The color is predominantly jet black, but a few specimens are banded mahogoney or rich brown. The terrain is flat and the scenery pleasant with a reed filled marsh to the south and the north.

At the south boundary of the site, which is about ten miles from where you first started in on the dirt road, are some shallow hills. In those hills jasper and agate can be found as well as more Apache tears. The material isn't overly plentiful, but there should be enough to make it worth the extra mileage. Be sure to take time to explore that region also. The agate and jasper seems to be concentrated in certain spots and virtually void in others, so, once you locate one piece, more is often nearby.

Specimens collected at Fish Valley Lake

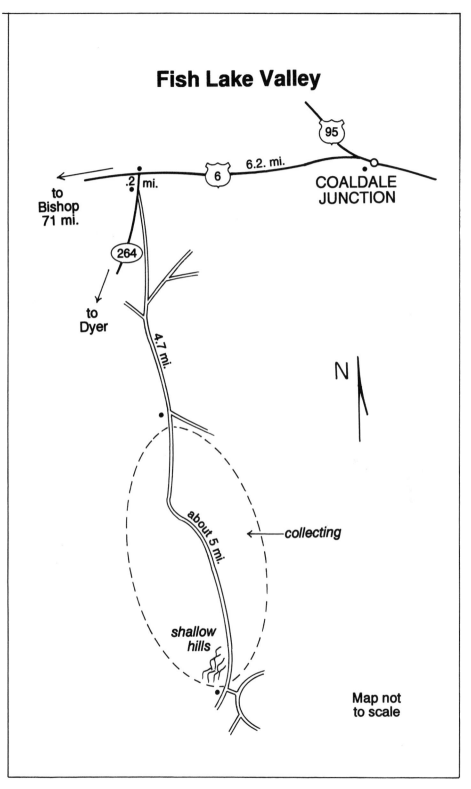

Fish Lake Valley

95

6.2. mi.

6

COALDALE
JUNCTION

to
Bishop
71 mi.

.2 mi.

264

to
Dyer

4.7 mi.

N

about 5 mi.

collecting

shallow
hills

Map not
to scale

COALDALE

The three locations discussed here offer rockhounds a variety of fine collectibles and some fascinating scenery to explore. To get to the first, labeled Site "A", take Highway 95 north from Coaldale Junction four and one-half miles and then turn east onto the dirt road heading towards the mountains. Proceed about nine-tenths of a mile and stop, that being the center of the first locality.

Site "A" offers bright red and orange jasper which is scattered randomly throughout the flatlands and areas of erosion for quite a distance. Size is somewhat small and quality tends to be only fair, but good specimens can be gathered with minimal effort.

Continue another one and four-tenths miles into the hills to the mine dumps where more agate and jasper can be picked up among the rubble, as can delicate selenite and quartz crystals. This is Site "B" and nothing is overly plentiful. However, the location offers a spectacular view of the valley below and that alone makes the additional mileage worthwhile.

Site "C" is, without a doubt, the most productive and interesting of the three. To get there, return to Coaldale Junction and head east six miles to where Highway 265 intersects. Instead of going south toward Silverpeak, however, follow the ruts heading north on the opposite side of the highway, two and one-half miles toward the unusual badlands-like hills. The road becomes very difficult to follow in places, and only the most rugged vehicles can make the trip. If you loose the tracks, just head towards the mounds. At the given mileage, you will encounter a deep wash, and it is there where you must stop. Scramble across the wash and hike into the badlands.

This is a geologically fascinating location, and jasper, agate, chalcedony and petrified wood can be found scattered randomly throughout it. Some is quite sizeable and the quality tends to be very good.

A view of scenic Site "C"

Coaldale

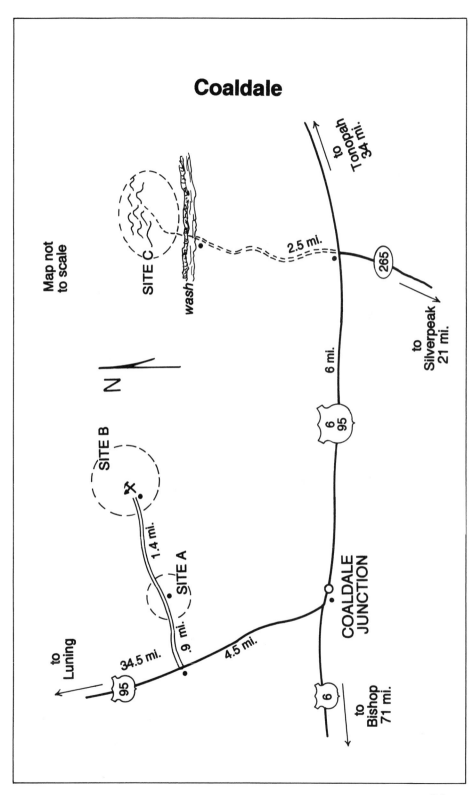

Map not to scale

SITE C

wash

2.5 mi.

265

to Tonopah 34 mi.

to Silverpeak 21 mi.

6 mi.

6 95

N

SITE B

SITE A

1.4 mi.

.9 mi.

to Luning

34.5 mi.

95

4.5 mi.

COALDALE JUNCTION

6

to Bishop 71 mi.

SODAVILLE

The hills just west of Sodaville provide rockhounds with a good selection of agate, jasper, selenite, petrified wood, and onyx. The jasper is especially colorful, occurring in shades of orange, red, yellow and black.

To get to Site "A", go four-tenths of a mile south of Sodaville on Highway 95 and then turn onto the dirt road leading west. Proceed one and four-tenths miles and then bear right on to the dim ruts heading into the hills. From that turn, continuing at least one-half mile further, agate and jasper can be found scattered all over. Four-wheel drive will probably be needed, but some other rugged vehicles might be able to make it the entire distance. Site"A" features an especially good concentration of the colorful jasper, and it is scattered all over the hillsides as shown on the map.

Site "B" is three-tenths of a mile from the main road and centered about a rock and debris covered hillside, easily seen on the right. Petrified wood can be found near the white onyx outcrop located directly under a basalt cap and it occurs in shades of brown, some being very nice. The onyx is generally plain white, with little banding or color contrasts, but some might be worth gathering.

Two-tenths of a mile further up are agate diggings. This is Site "C". You will need a pick, shovel, gloves, goggles, small sledge hammer, gads and chisels in order to get anything except chips. Fine tumbling size material can be obtained from the surface.

Site"D" boasts interesting selenite slabs, and is reached by returning to the main dirt road and going seven-tenths of a mile toward an easily spotted mine. Collect in and around the dumps unless it appears the mine is no longer abandoned. If that is the case, do not trespass and restrict collecting to regions outside its boundaries.

Sodaville

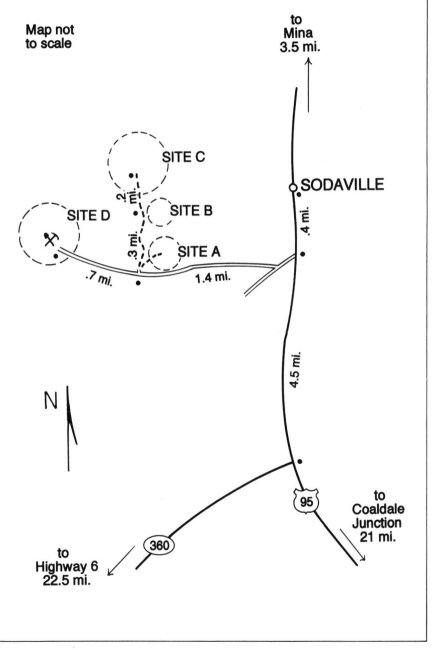

Map not to scale

to
Mina
3.5 mi.

SITE C

SITE D

.2 mi.

SITE B

.3 mi.

SODAVILLE

.4 mi.

SITE A

.7 mi.

1.4 mi.

4.5 mi.

N

95

360

to
Coaldale
Junction
21 mi.

to
Highway 6
22.5 mi.

CROW SPRINGS APACHE TEARS

This is an interesting collecting area near the once bustling stage stop of Crow Springs. Crow Springs served as an intermediate rest area for the Humphrey-Esner Stage Line which connected Sodaville and Tonopah. It featured a boarding house, homes for the employees, corrals, saloon, restaurant and a large barn. At one time, hundreds of meals were served there each day, not only to passengers riding the stagecoach, but to the countless wagon drivers transporting supplies between the two cities. Crow Springs Stage Station closed in 1904 when the Tonopah railroad was completed, and little now remains of the historic Nevada site.

Not far from Crow Springs' crumbling adobe walls is a locality of interest to mineral collectors which features a seemingly unlimited supply of tiny, glass-like Apache tears. To get to the site, travel six and nine-tenths miles west of Millers Rest Area on Highway 6 as illustrated on the map. Turn north onto the dirt road and proceed six and eight-tenths more miles. At that point, go right and continue another eight-tenths of a mile to the obsidianite field. The tears tend to be of high quality and the quantity seems unlimited. Simply park and explore the surrounding terrain. The black tears are easy to spot, since they contrast markedly with the lighter colored native soil.

There are a number of turquoise mines in the hills about a mile further north, but most are protected by valid claims and off limits to collectors. Exploring some of the washes below those mines, though, occasionally rewards diligent rockhounds with some small, but colorful chips of that semiprecious gemstone.

Apache tears collected at the site

Crow Springs

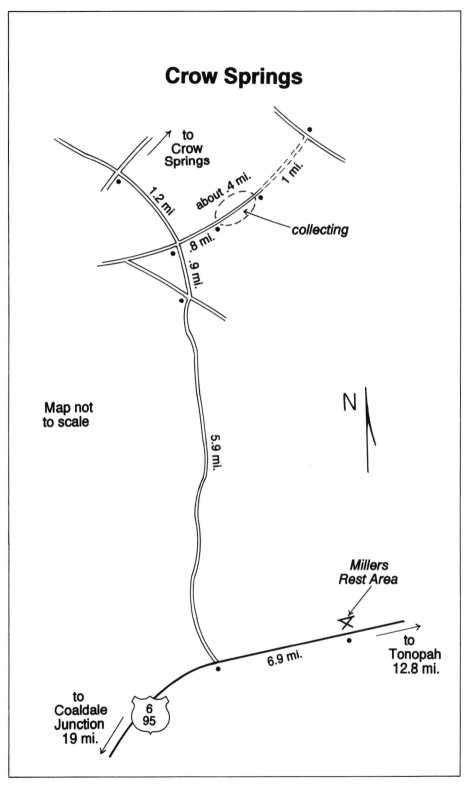

to
Crow
Springs

1.2 mi

about .4 mi.

1 mi.

.8 mi.

.9 mi.

collecting

Map not
to scale

5.9 mi.

N

Millers
Rest Area

to
Tonopah
12.8 mi.

6.9 mi.

to
Coaldale
Junction
19 mi.

6
95

TONOPAH JASPER

Tonopah is known as the "Queen of the Nevada Silver Camps" due to the fact that over $200,000,000 in precious metals, mostly silver, have been extracted from its mines. The original lode was discovered by Jim Butler, who, while prospecting in 1900, got mad and picked up a stone to throw at his burrow. The stone felt particulary heavy, though, and he became suspicious that it might possess a high metallic concentration. His suspicions proved valid, and the rest is history.

Virtually all the silver mines are completely off limits to collectors, but there is one region northeast of town that offers rockhounds a good opportunity to gather colorful jasper, as well as agate and petrified wood. To get there, take Highway 6 east from town about six miles to Highway 376. From there go north one and one-half miles to where a flat area will be seen on the left, with mountains further beyond. That marks the center of the site, and it extends quite a distance in all directions, on both sides of the highway.

Park well off the pavement and start hiking, keeping a keen eye to the ground. The best collecting seems to be towards the mountains, with the wood being most abundant in the foothills. Jasper tends to be the most plentiful of the region's minerals, with sizes averaging about an inch across.

Be patient and willing to do some walking and your rockhounding trek through this mineralogically fascinating region should be very productive and enjoyable.

Tonopah

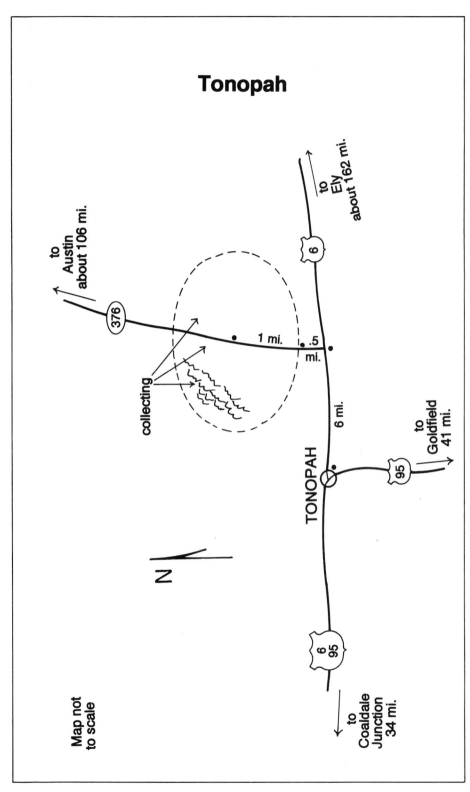

to
Austin
about 106 mi.

376

1 mi.   .5
         mi.

collecting

to
Ely
about 162 mi.

6

TONOPAH

6 mi.

to
Goldfield
41 mi.

95

6
95

to
Coaldale
Junction
34 mi.

N

Map not
to scale

Chert, agate, petrified wood and jasper
Lake Lahontan

Wonderstone-Wonderstone Mountain

Japser and agate-Middle Gate

Silver Springs selenite

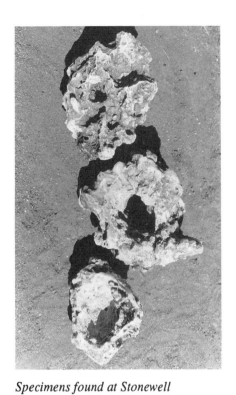

Specimens found at Stonewell

Obsidian and other minerals-Basalt

Agate and petrified wood-Lida

Lake Mead agate and other collectibles

GOLDFIELD GEM CLAIM

Apache tears, fortification jasp-agate, bull's-eye agate, chalcedony, dendritic agate, rainbow agate and opalite, in a multitude of colors, can all be found at this location, which is generally regarded as one of Nevada's premier fee rockhounding sites. Some of the most interesting and colorful jasper and jasp-agate to be found anywhere can be obtained here, and most is solid and takes an excellent polish. This is a private claim and open nearly all year, but the schedule tends to be somewhat irregular.

To get there, go two and four-tenths miles north from Goldfield on Highway 95 to where a sign will be seen on the left side of the roadway. If the "open" banner is not posted, you may be out of luck. Turn west and follow the mine sign to the office. Do not, under any circumstances, start collecting without first reporting in and making arrangements.

After checking in, the owner, Mr. Earl Nesser, will escort you to the best areas, depending upon what you want. It seems that the entire mountain is made of top quality, immensely colorful cutting material. You can either extract it directly from the hillside with hardrock tools, or, if you don't have enough energy, tons of outstanding specimens can be picked up off the ground and from tables at the office. Fees, at time of publication, range from $1.00 to $4.00 per pound, depending on how much you gather and how many people are in your group.

This is open desert country and Mr. Nesser has primitive restrooms, but no water or wood. There is no charge for camping and visitors are welcome to spend one day or a week, with no obligation to purchase anything.

Due to the unpredictability in regards to hours of operation, it is highly recommended that you write well ahead of your planned visit to make certain somebody will be there. Since Mr. Messner only gets into town a few times a month, it often takes quite a while to receive a response. The address is P.O. Box 495, Goldfield, Nevada 89013.

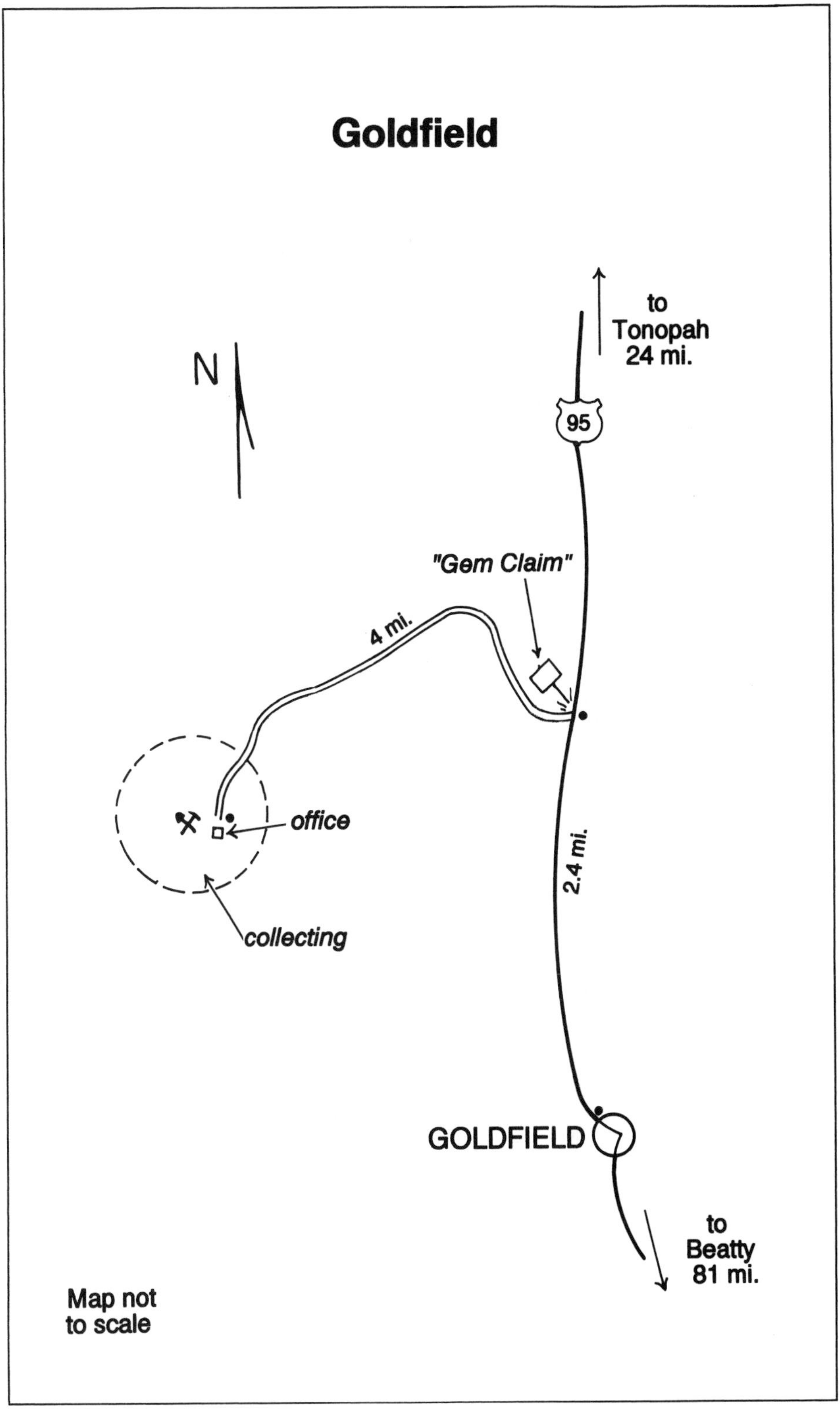

Goldfield

N

to
Tonopah
24 mi.

95

"Gem Claim"

4 mi.

office

collecting

2.4 mi.

GOLDFIELD

to
Beatty
81 mi.

Map not
to scale

STONEWALL AGATE

The two sites illustrated on the map offer collectors agate, chalcedony and opalite, some of which is very unusual. Site "A" is situated just off Highway 95, one and seven-tenths miles north from where Highway 266 intersects. At that mileage, go east two-tenths of a mile, closing the gate after having passed through, and bear left another one-tenth of a mile, and then go right at the fork, approximately two-tenths of a mile toward the light colored hills, as shown. From there, and continuing for at least another one-half mile, lots of agate and petrified wood can be found scattered throughout the lowlands, all the way to the hills.

Just park and start walking. Some of the agate is very contorted and bubbly, but occurs in often sizeable chunks. Even though it is not especially colorful, such pieces make very interesting polished slabs. The wood tends to be specimen quality, rather than cutting grade, but it is still worth gathering.

To get to Site "B", go south on Highway 95, one and one-half miles from where the road to Site "A" intersected. Look for a stop sign on the east. That marks the place that you should turn. Go about one and nine-tenths miles and park near the conspicuous gray hills. As was the case at the previous site, these badland-like geological formations seem to be indicators of potentially good collecting.

Rockhounds can pick up lots of nice agate, chalcedony, and petrified wood, most of which is very similar to that found at Site "A". Just do some hiking from the road, and it won't take long before you are able to gather a good quantity of fine cutting and specimen material.

Parked at Site "B"

Stonewall Agate

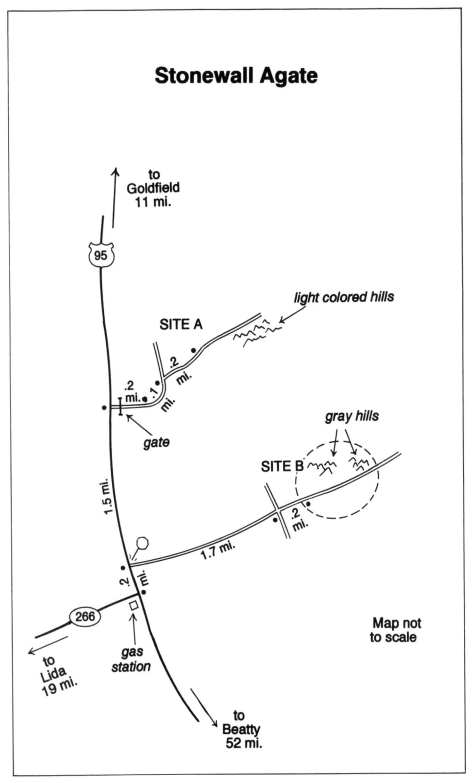

to
Goldfield
11 mi.

95

light colored hills

SITE A

.2
mi.

.2
mi. .1
mi.

gate

1.5 mi.

gray hills

SITE B

.2
mi.

1.7 mi.

266

.2 mi.

Map not
to scale

gas
station

to
Lida
19 mi.

to
Beatty
52 mi.

LIDA WOOD AND AGATE

This somewhat remote location provides a great spot to obtain agate, chalecdony and petrified wood. To get there, go south on Highway 95 three and four-tenths miles from where Highway 266 intersects. At that point, a cattle guard will be seen, just off the pavement, and it is there that you should turn southeast toward the gray badland-like hills in the distance. A fork and windmill will be encountered at the seven-tenths of a mile mark, and you should bear right, continuing straight ahead.

Another three and seven-tenths miles along the way will place you at an intersection where it is necessary to turn left. After going only a few tenths of a mile, the road starts to deteriorate rapidly, with the final one and one-half miles being extremely rough and deeply rutted. Be advised that it is impossible for anything except high clearance, rugged vehicles to traverse the final stretch. Do not drive any further than your vehicle is capable of going. Park when it gets treacherous, and walk the remaining distance. Agate, wood and chalcedony can be found scattered throughout the lower foothills, so it should prove very fruitful to make the hike.

Once you have come about six miles in from the highway, you will be at the edge of this photogenic, extensive and productive collecting area. The rockhounding continues throughout the gray hills and the lower regions to their east, and it shouldn't take long before finding a good quantity of quality specimens. Don't hesitate to do some walking, and pay particularly close attention to regions of erosion and low lying areas where material may have been washed during heavy rainstorms.

Parked at the collecting site

Lida

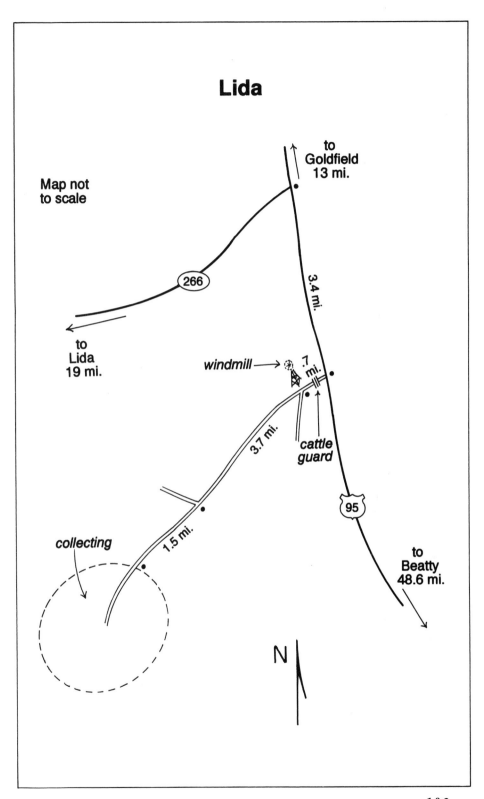

Map not to scale

266

to Lida
19 mi.

to Goldfield
13 mi.

3.4 mi.

windmill →

.7 mi.

cattle guard

3.7 mi.

1.5 mi.

95

collecting

to Beatty
48.6 mi.

N

SCOTTY'S JUNCTION APACHE TEARS

This site boasts a seemingly unlimited supply of tiny, but frequently gem quality, Apache tears. Without a doubt, it is one of the most accessible of all sites discussed in this book, being alongside a major, well paved highway.

To get there, take Highway 95 eight miles south from Scotty's Junction and park well off the pavement. The field of obsidianites is extensive, so don't hesitate to do some hiking on either side of the road for as far as you feel like going. The tears seem to be randomly scattered, so if the particular spot you first explore doesn't seem to have much, just drive a few tenths of a mile further south or north to try again. Be very careful if you cross the highway, since cars often travel at very high speeds through here, not expecting pedestrians on the pavement.

The best time of day to search for Apache tears is in the late afternoon or early morning, when the sun's ray are at a low angle. At that time, walk with the sun to your back and the tears will sparkle in the sunlight, making them very easy to spot. Be sure to take a bucket, cup or other type container for gathering your little gemstones.

Collecting off Highway 95 at the site

Scotty's Junction

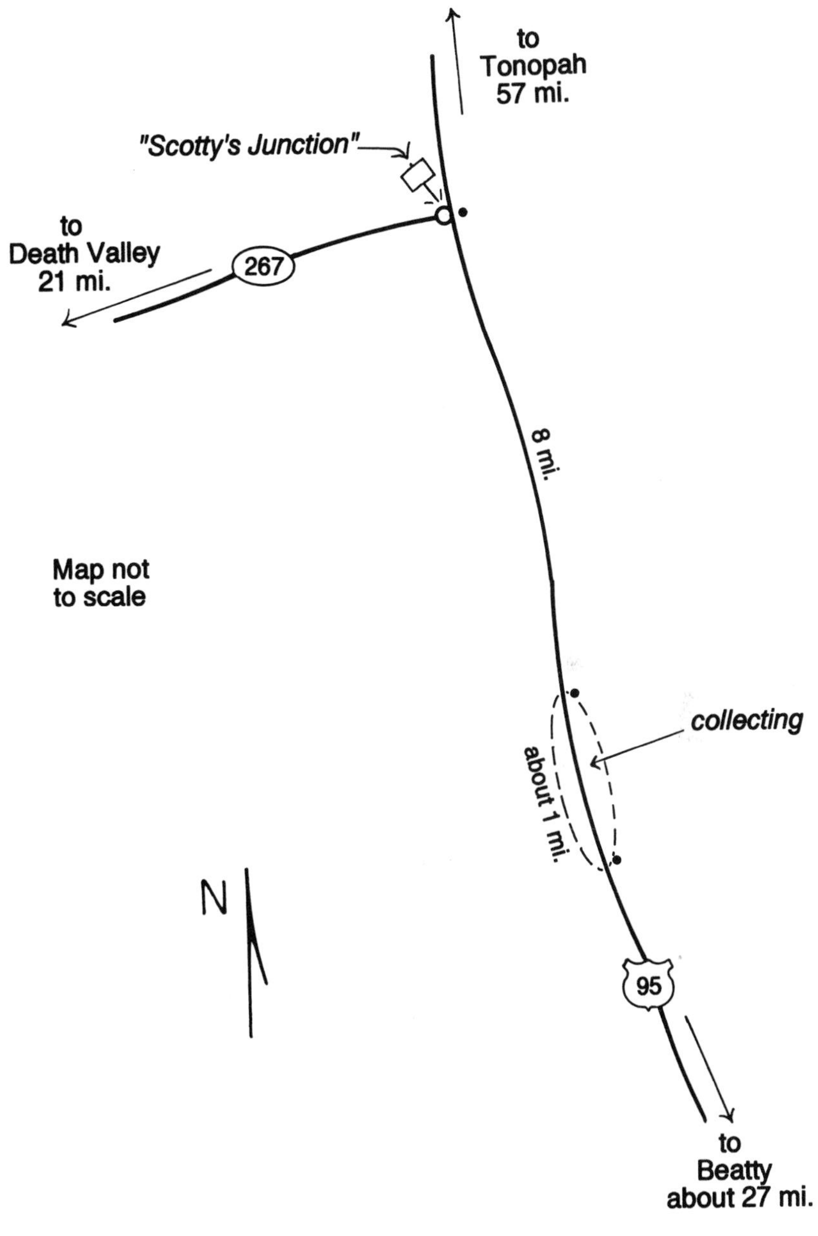

to
Tonopah
57 mi.

"Scotty's Junction"

to
Death Valley
21 mi.

267

8 mi.

Map not
to scale

collecting

about 1 mi.

N

95

to
Beatty
about 27 mi.

MEIKLEJOHN PEAK FOSSILS

Fossilized specimens of Ordovician crinoids, sponges, trilobites, barnacles and other ancient forms of sea life can be gathered just south of Beatty. To get to this fascinating location, take Highway 95 south from town one and three-tenths miles to where a cattle guard will be seen to the east. Turn there, proceed four and two-tenths miles up the hill, and then go right another nine-tenths of a mile. At that point, steep ruts will be encountered leading off to the left and you should follow them another two-tenths of a mile to the flat parking area. The balance of the trip must be made on foot, making this a collecting site only for those who are physically fit and willing to work for their finds.

The actual limestone deposit which contains the 475 million year old inhabitants of this region is situated high on the mountainside and is very hazardous and difficult to get to. By hiking up the dim trail into the canyon as shown on the map, lots of fossil bearing material will be found strewn throughout the canyon floor. Look for limestone whose surface is lumpy or uneven; that irregularity probably has been caused by embedded fossils. Any suspect chunk should be examined up close, and, if you are patient, it shouldn't take long to find quite a number of fine samples.

Most of the fossils are found in the gray and greenish-gray, layered limestone, and it will probably be worth your time to examine all such material. Since the specimens seem to be fully replaced with silica, it is possible to dissolve all or part of the host limestone away in acid. If you do use acid, however, be certain you know exactly what you are doing and be very careful.

Hiking from the parking area into the fossil bearing canyon

Meiklejohn Peak

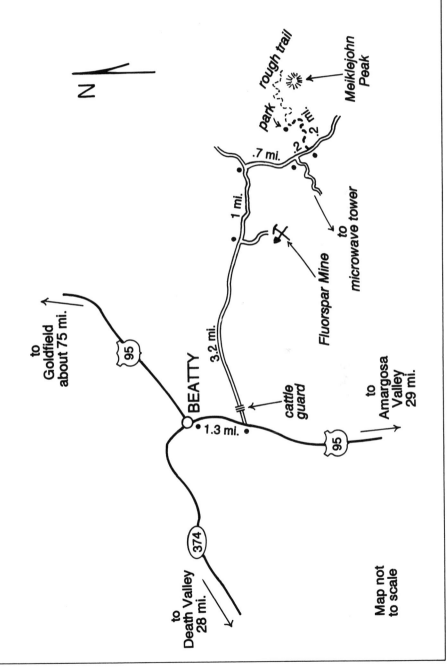

rough trail

park

Meiklejohn Peak

.2

.2

.7 mi.

1 mi.

to microwave tower

Fluorspar Mine

3.2 mi.

to Goldfield about 75 mi.

95

BEATTY

cattle guard

to Amargosa Valley 29 mi.

95

1.3 mi.

374

to Death Valley 28 mi.

N

Map not to scale

CARRARA MARBLE

Good quality, bright, white marble can be obtained in the mountains southeast of Beatty. To get to this interesting and productive location, go south on Highway 95 exactly seven miles from where Highway 374 intersects in town. At that point, there is a stop sign at a dirt road leading toward the mountains on the left. This is where you should turn and proceed two and six-tenths miles to the easily observed mine in the foothills. Along the way you will pass the ruins of the small town of Carrara, where nothing more than foundations now remain. The last half mile is steep and rocky, limiting access to only the most rugged vehicles. If you have any doubts as to whether you can make that final part of the journey, park when the road gets too rugged and hike the remaining distance.

Marble can be found all over the road as you approach the quarry, but most is very plain, with little or no discernable banding or color contrasts. Some, however, does disply subtle bands, and, when such pieces are polished, the results are very pleasing.

Be sure to allow enough time to adequately explore this intriguing site. Since the quality varies greatly, it will take some patient searching to obtain the best it has to offer. Using hardrock tools in the quarry itself may prove to be fruitful, but if you choose to do that, be very careful not to knock loose anything from above. Attacking the marble directly is arduous work. Unless you come upon an especially nice deposit, it would probably be more productive just to sort through the tons of material scattered over the surrounding landscape, dumps and road.

There are additional nearby marble mines which can be spotted as you drive in. If you have time, it might be worthwhile to explore those prospects also. Always remember, when collecting on mine dumps, however, that ownership status changes. Be sure, when you visit, to ascertain whether or not it is open to collectors. Do not gather minerals at any mine or quarry which is not abandoned.

Carrara Marble

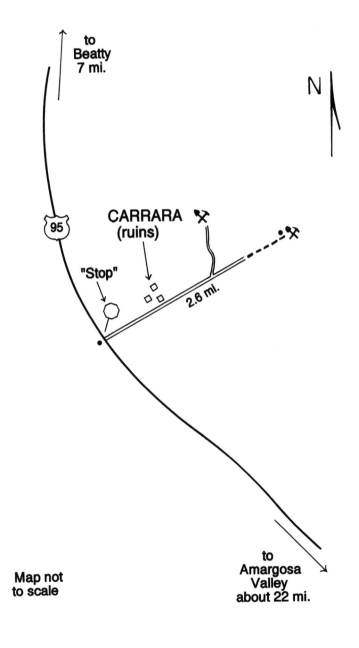

to
Beatty
7 mi.

N

95

CARRARA
(ruins)

"Stop"

2.6 mi.

to
Amargosa
Valley
about 22 mi.

Map not
to scale

HENDERSON AMETHYSTINE

The two locations illustrated on the accompanying map afford rockhounds with a variety of interesting collectibles, including carving stone, amethystine, green jasper, agate and selenite.

To get to the sites, go east on Highway 147 three miles from where it intersects the Boulder Highway in Henderson. At that point, there is a stop sign on the right, that being where you should turn. Go eight-tenths of a mile, bear right at road's end, and proceed another four-tenths of a mile along the ridge and down the hill. From there, turn left one-tenth of a mile then right up the hill, traveling about two-tenths of a mile to the easily seen diggings on the left. This is Site"A".

Here, rockhounds can gather colorful, but scarce, agate which tends to be scattered throughout the surrounding hillsides. Much of this material is filled with nice black dendrites and can be used to produce fascinating cabochons and other polished pieces. In addition, a white carving stone and some delicate, purple amethystine can be unearthed by digging in the pits. Some of the excavations have been tunneled, as rockhounds followed a good seam, but it is very unsafe to crawl under any earthen overhang. For that reason, rather than expanding the tunnels, it is advisable to spend time breaking them down and digging from an open pit.

To get to Site "B", return to Racetrack Road, as shown, and go south eight-tenths of a mile, then left onto Geneva Road another six-tenths of a mile. Just past the power line tower, turn right, and travel about one-tenth of a mile into the gully where diggings can be spotted on both sides. It is here that green, jade-like jasper can be obtained, some filled with interesting black inclusions. In addition delicate selenite crystals can be found "growing" from the soft soil and a low-grade agate can also be found scattered randomly throughout the canyon and adjacent hillsides. Just about all minerals from here are somewhat weathered and/or porous, thereby not conducive to accepting good polish. For that reason, allow sufficient time to find the best the site has to offer.

A view of some of the diggings at Site "B"

Henderson

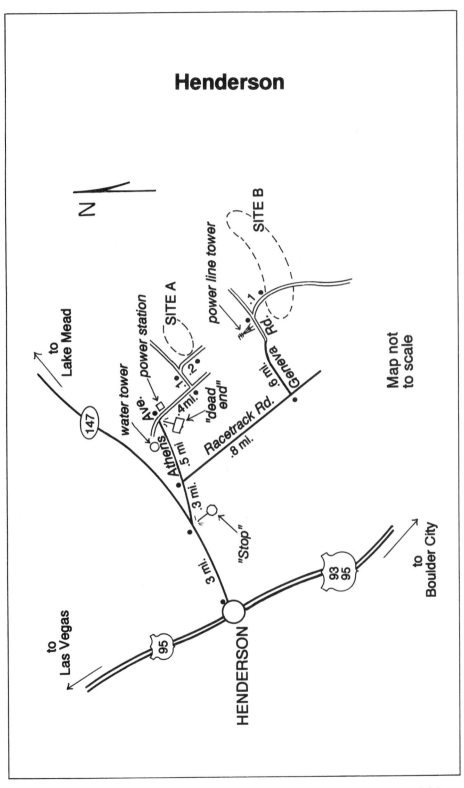

THREE KIDS MINE MINERALS

Bright green jasper, onyx and selenite are just a few of the nice minerals obtainable in the region surrounding the Three Kids Mine, a few miles east of Henderson. To get there, take Highway 147 five and two-tenths miles east from where the Boulder Highway intersects and turn right onto the ruts just past the Rod and Reel general store. The mine dumps can easily be seen as you approach, but it is difficult to miss the access road unless you are looking for it.

Go about two-tenths of a mile to the foundations, which are situated at the edge of the colossal pit. The onyx and selenite can be found throughout the boulders on the upper dumps, but be very careful when exploring there, since it could be dangerous, especially if you try to get specimens near or beyond the edge. There are lots of large, banded onyx boulders all over, and some contain portions which are highly desirable. It will take sledge hammers, gads and chisels to remove those portions, but the work will be rewarded.

This is an interesting and photogenic spot to explore, but be advised that there is lots of extremely fine black, insidious dirt all over the dump area, making it very likely that you will conclude your visit considerably more soiled than when you arrived. Do not venture into the pit, and if it appears that the mine is no longer abandoned, do not collect any minerals.

From the mine looking east, a faint trail can be seen climbing the ridge in the saddle. Hike that trail to the top of the hill, and in the saddle, you will be able to find diggings where previous collectors have gathered a beautiful green jasper known locally as "Henderson jade". Much of that jade-like material takes a good polish, making the hike worth the effort . If you do make the trek, be sure to take some extra water, and avoid hiking during the scorching heat of summer. Save this trip for a cooler part of the year.

Three Kids Mine

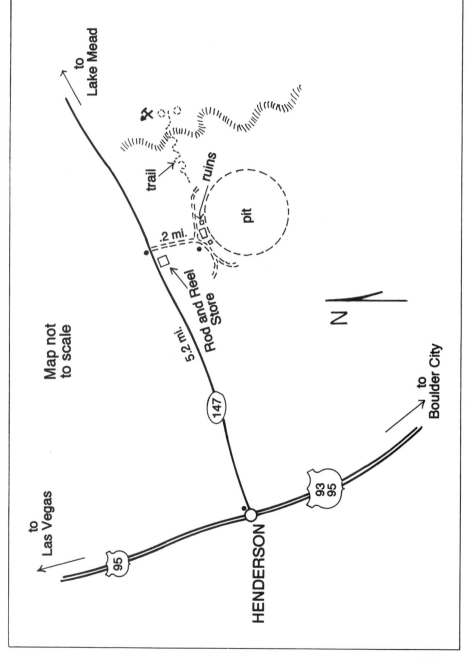

Map not to scale

to Lake Mead

trail

ruins

pit

.2 mi.

5.2 mi.

Rod and Reel Store

147

N

to Boulder City

93 95

HENDERSON

95

to Las Vegas

113

LAKE MEAD AGATE

Lots of nice, and often sizeable chunks of agate can be gathered through the territory north of Lake Mead. Two spots, in particular, are especially productive. The first, labeled Site "A" on the map, is reached by taking North Shore Road three and six-tenths miles from where Highway 147 intersects. At that point, there is a conspicuous orange butte on the right side of the road, and just beyond is Montana Agate Road. Turn right and go about two-tenths of a mile to the beginning of this extensive site. Simply park well off the roadway and hike in either direction, keeping an eye out for selenite, jasper and agate. The agate is especially nice here, some displaying delicate lace patterns, while other samples are filled with interesting and often colorful inclusions of every imaginable shape and variety. There is also some incredibly beautiful, shimmering, deep violet agate to be found here, and it is considered a real prize.

Brilliant red jasper can also be picked up, as can occasional chunks of petrified wood. Nothing is overly concentrated in any one place, so it is necessary to do some exploring in order to gather acceptable quantites.

Site "B" is similar to Site "A", but doesn't seem to offer quite as much. It is, however, still worth the stop since it is so close. To get there, return to North Shore Road, and continue east another one and four-tenths miles to 8.0 Road. Turn right, and go about two-tenths of a mile to the start of the site. As was the case before, hike the flatlands and low hills, looking for agate, jasper and petrified wood. About one and two-tenths miles from the pavement are some gray hills, on the east, where nice selenite crystals can be gathered from the soft soil.

Parked in Site "A"

Lake Mead

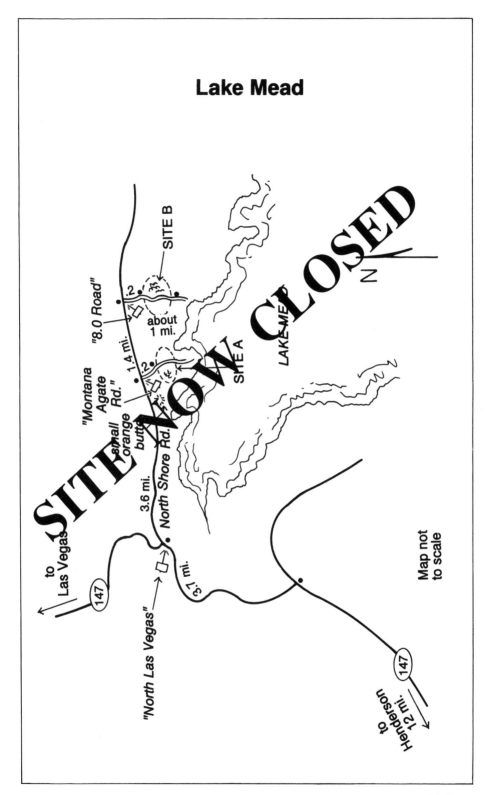

SITE NOW CLOSED

SITE B

"8.0 Road"

about 1 mi.

1.4 mi.

"Montana Agate Rd."

small orange butte

SITE A

LAKE MEAD

North Shore Rd.

3.6 mi.

to Las Vegas

147

"North Las Vegas"

3.7 mi.

N

Map not to scale

147

to Henderson 12 mi.

115

MINERAL INDEX

AGATE
- Basalt
- Bell Canyon
- Black Rock
- Bogwood Diggings
- Buffalo Canyon
- Cedarville
- Coaldale
- Fernley
- Fish Lake Valley
- Gabbs
- Goldfield
- Green Mountain
- Henderson
- Lake Lahontan
- Lake Mead
- Lida
- Lovelock
- Mcdermitt II
- McDermitt III
- Middle Gate
- Monte Cristo
- Silver Springs
- Sodaville
- Stonewell
- The Sump
- Texas Spring
- Tonopah
- Trinity Mountains

AMETHYSTINE
- Henderson

APACHE TEARS
- Big Springs
- Crow Springs
- Denio
- Fish Lake Valley
- Gabbs
- Goldfield
- Scotty's Junction
- The Sump
- Vya to Gerlach

ARROW HEADS
- Black Rock
- Nellie Springs

BLOODSTONE
- Cedarville South

BOGWOOD
- Bogwood Diggings

CARNELIAN
- Denio

CHALCEDONY
- Bell Canyon
- Coaldale
- Gabbs
- Lida
- Middle Gate
- Stonewell
- The Sump

CHERT
- Lake Lahontan
- McDermitt II

CHRYSOCOLLA
- Contact

COMMON OPAL
- Buffalo Canyon
- Denio
- Trinity Mountains

FOSSILS
- Buffalo Canyon
- Meiklejohn Peak

GALENA
- Quartz Mountain

GARNETS
- Garnet Hill

GEODES
- Bell Canyon
- Black Rock
- Contact
- Middle Gate
- Rabbit Springs

JASP-AGATE
- Goldfield
- Palisade

MINERAL INDEX

JASPER
  Basalt
  Bell Canyon
  Black Rock
  Buffalo Canyon
  Coaldale
  Fish Lake Valley
  Gabbs
  Goldfield
  Green Mountain
  Henderson
  Lake Lahontan
  Lake Mead
  McDermitt II
  McDermitt III
  Middle Gate
  Monte Cristo
  Nellie Springs
  Palisade
  Sodaville
  Silver Springs
  The Sump
  Three Kids Mine
  Tonopah

LIMB CASTS
  Bogwood Diggings
  The Sump
  Texas Spring

MALACHITE
  Contact

MARBLE
  Carrara

MOONSTONE
  Big Springs

NODULES
  Middle Gate
  Rabbit Springs
  Trinity Mountains

OBSIDIAN
  Basalt
  Big Springs
  Davis creek
  Nellie Springs
  Vya to Gerlach

ONYX
  Jackpot
  Sodaville
  Three Kids Mine

OPALITE
  Bell Canyon
  Buffalo Canyon
  Denio
  Goldfield
  Lovelock
  Nellie Springs
  Stonewell
  The Sump
  Vya to Gerlach

OPALIZED WOOD
  Gabbs

PETRIFIED WOOD
  Basalt
  Black Rock
  Bogwood Diggings
  Cedarville
  Cedarville South
  Coaldale
  Daisy Creek
  Gabbs
  Goldfield
  Hubbard Basin
  Lake Lahontan
  Lake Mead
  Lida
  Lovelock
  McDermitt II
  McDermitt III
  Monte Cristo
  Nellie Springs
  Quartz Mountain
  Sodaville
  The Sump
  Tonopah
  Trinity Mountains
  Vya to Gerlach

PINK FELDSPAR
  Gabbs

MINERAL INDEX

PRECIOUS OPAL
    Black Rock
    Rainbow Ridge
    Royal Peacock
    Trinity Mountains

PYRITE
    Quartz Mountain

QUARTZ
    Coaldale
    Deep Springs
    Quartz Mountain

RHYOLITE
    Bell Canyon
    Garnet Hill
    Trinity Mountains

SELENITE
    Coaldale
    Henderson
    Lake Mead
    Silver Springs
    Soadville
    The Sump
    Three Kids Mine

WONDERSTONE
    Bell Canyon
    Green Mountain
    McDermitt I
    McDermitt II
    Wonderstone

Buffalo Canyon fossil

Other related books by Gem Guides Book Co.